# "church bulletin bits" #1

# "church bulletin bits"

volume #1

GEORGE W. KNIGHT
COMPILER

BAKER BOOK HOUSE
Grand Rapids, Michigan 49506

*Copyright 1976 by*
*Baker Book House Company*
*ISBN: 0-8010-5368-4*
*Printed in the United States of America*

*Thirteenth printing, May 1990*

# Contents

# Preface

The most-asked question around a church office must be, "How do I fill that empty space on page 3?" It is posed practically every week as busy secretaries and ministers of education put the finishing touches on the church newsletter.

This book is designed to provide a very practical answer to that very practical question. Here is a supply of short paragraphs and fillers that can be used as needed, conveniently arranged under eighteen different headings.

As compiler of this book, I claim no originality for any of the entries. Most are of anonymous authorship, and many have passed from bulletin to bulletin for so many years that they have become "classics" in the field. I combed hundreds of bulletins from scores of churches for three years to find the two hundred fillers that appear here.

In those few cases where the author is known, his name is included. Many thanks to these persons as well as the scores of anonymous writers who challenge us through these short paragraphs to put Christ and His church first in our lives.

Nothing will kill a good story like repeating it too often. Church newsletter editors can avoid overusing these fillers by using the convenient Record of Publication in the back of this book. Then with one quick glance the editor can tell what items have already been published and when.

If there is such a thing as a religious book that is designed to be used rather than read or talked about, this is it. I hope it will help our churches produce church bulletins and newsletters with a little more spice and variety.

GEORGE W. KNIGHT

# 1
# Church Attendance and Support

---

## 1. CHECKUP FOR CHURCH MEMBERS

How many morning services would we have if everyone would stay home when I do?

How often would the evening service be canceled if no one would go except when I do?

How often would the Sunday school meet if others would attend only when I do?

How much Christian instruction would the children of my community receive if other parents would pay only as much attention to it as I do?

How many neighbors would be invited to services and welcomed if others would invite and welcome only as many people as I do?

How many prayers would be offered for my pastor, my neighbors, and my church if others would pray only as much as I do?

How many words of testimony would be given for Christ if others would speak out for Christ only as much as I do?

What kind of church would my church be if every member were just like me?

## 2. I BELIEVE IN THE CHURCH

I believe more profoundly in the church every hour that I live. A man can make his testimony go further through the church than through any independent movements. He can make his money, his testimony, and all his work go further. He can do more constructive work through the church than any other way in the world. That is my deepest conviction. I have watched all kinds of independent movements, and my conviction steadily deepens that a Christian is doing the wisest thing possible when he links his life with the church.

*—George W. Truett*

## 3. TEN THINGS MY CHURCH PROVIDES FOR ME

1. Christian worship through which I learn to practice the presence of God.
2. Christian preaching with its spiritual instruction and its challenge to holy living.
3. Christian ordinances, baptism and the Lord's Supper, which are continual reminders of the possibility of abundant new life through surrender to God and daily communion with Him.
4. Christian instruction through which I learn to think high thoughts and discover spiritual truths.
5. Christian fellowship which will strengthen the best that is in me.
6. Christian evangelistic opportunities through which I can make my life count for God.
7. Christian training opportunities through which I can find myself and grow in the Christian life.
8. Christian service opportunities through which I can make my life more useful to God and humanity.

9. Christian missions through which I can make my influence for good felt throughout the world.
10. Christian stewardship opportunities through which I can express my gratitude to God for His grace in my life.

## 4. THE POWER OF AN INVITATION

On Monday a friend met me on the street. "I noticed you were absent from our civic club's last meeting," he said. "Will you be there next Wednesday?"

"No," I replied. "I can't make it. Don't look for me."

Two men asked me on Tuesday if I could come. I said to the first, "I wish I could, but I can't this week." The next one I answered, "My schedule looks impossible, but I'll try to find the time to come."

Wednesday morning in the post office a fourth man asked if I would be at the meeting that day. "I'll try to come," I replied, "but I may not make it." Before I got to my car, a fifth man stopped me, and I promised I would be there for sure.

I don't know whose official duty it was to contact me, but I couldn't resist the invitation from five different men. We all like to go where we are wanted.

If you want the unsaved, the indifferent, and absentees to attend our church, you must let them know. They know that if you really want them to come, you will find the opportunity to invite them. This is a task for every member of our church.

## 5. EIGHT MYSTERIES AT OUR CHURCH

1. The mystery of the empty pew. The freedom to worship apparently is interpreted as freedom from worship.
2. The mystery of the disappearing church member. Some move and disappear without a trace. No one knows where they live.

11

3. The mystery of the unaccompanied child. Many children are sent along with other children and dropped off by a parent who does not attend Sunday school and church services himself.
4. The mystery of the closed Bible. In many homes the Bible is left on a table or shelf to gather dust. It is not allowed to speak to the family, which needs its message each day.
5. The mystery of the buried talents. Many of our church members have the ability to serve; yet they hide their talents, refusing to use them for God.
6. The mystery of the uncommitted dollar. How does a person who professes faith in Christ get everything converted but his pocketbook?
7. The mystery of the grumbling saint. With so much going for him, how can the Christian develop a griping, complaining attitude?
8. The mystery of the misused day. Some Christians use a beautiful Sunday for everything except the worship and praise of God.

## 6. ALL SYSTEMS GO

Hold this rectangle to your face and blow on it. If it turns green, call your physician. If it turns brown, see your dentist. If it turns purple, consult your psychiatrist. If it turns red, see your banker. If it turns black, call your lawyer and make a will.

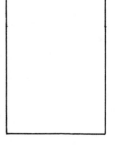

If it remains the same color, you're in good health and there is no reason on earth why you should not be in church next Sunday morning!

## 7. YOUR CHURCH IS YOU

You are a walking advertisement of your church and the Christ whom it proclaims. You take the church out of its four walls and make it live in the everyday affairs of life. In fact, what people think of your church, they think of you.

Some have the idea that the pastor is the church. It is true that the pastor often speaks for the church, declares what it stands for, and invites people into its fellowship. It is his job to know the church's business and to act in its behalf. He is your representative, but he certainly is not your substitute.

The preaching in the pulpit is fruitless unless it is reflected in the lives of members of the congregation. Classroom teaching is ineffective unless it comes to life in the attitudes and behavior of the people. Your church is measured not so much by what its leaders say as by what you do. It is easy to make speeches and claims, but claims must be validated by the product. You are your church's product and the validation of its claims. You are the means by which the good life advocated by the church is communicated to people.

Your church professes a concern for people; you express that concern in the way you act toward others. Your church tries to build up a Christian world; you validate these attempts by your conduct on the job or in your community. Your church claims to have a gospel that will make people new, opening to them a more satisfying life; you are the demonstration of that claim.

Your daily acts as a Christian preach more sermons, teach more people, and save more lives than the words that are spoken inside the four walls of your church building. You are a cell of the living church. Without you, the church has no life.

## 8. DEAD WEIGHT IN THE CHURCH

*I've been a dead weight many years*
*Around the church's neck;*
*I've let the others carry me*
*And always pay the check.*

*I've had my name upon the rolls*
*For years and years gone by;*

*I've criticized and grumbled, too;*
*Nothing could satisfy.*

*I've been a dead weight long enough*
*Upon the church's back;*
*Beginning now, I'm going to take*
*A wholly different track.*

*I'm going to pray and pay and work*
*And carry loads instead;*
*And not have others carry me*
*As people do the dead.*

## 9. JOHN DOESN'T BELONG TO OUR CHURCH

Someone asked a pastor if a certain man called John belonged to his church. "No, John doesn't belong to our church," the pastor replied, "but his name is on our roll." The inquirer, a little confused by this answer, asked the difference between belonging to the church and having one's name on the roll.

"It's like this," the pastor explained. "John's time doesn't belong to the church; neither do his talents, his energy, or his money."

"What sort of membership does John have in your church?" asked the other man.

"It's a bit difficult to explain," the pastor said. "Since he seldom comes to the church, he has no feeling of belonging to the church family. The church has never become a spiritual home to him. It would be stretching a point to say that John belongs to the church."

"To be perfectly honest, I guess there isn't an ounce of John that truly belongs to the church."

## 10. MORBUS SABBATICUS (SUNDAY SICKNESS)

Morbus Sabbaticus is a disease peculiar to church members. Here are some of its symptoms:

14

1. It never interferes with the appetite.
2. It never lasts more than twenty-four hours at a time.
3. No physician is ever called.
4. It always proves fatal in the end—to the soul.
5. It is contagious.

The attack usually comes on suddenly every Sunday. No ill effects are felt on Saturday night, and the patient awakes as usual, feeling fine. He eats a hearty breakfast. About 9 A.M. the attack comes on, and it lasts until around noon.

In the afternoon the patient is much improved. He is able to take a ride and read the Sunday newspaper. The patient eats a hearty supper, but the attack comes on again and lasts through the evening. The patient is able to go to work Monday, as usual.

## 11. FOOTBALL GAMES ARE NOT FOR ME

I've made up my mind never to attend another football game. I've been an avid football fan for many years, but now I've had it. Let me list the reasons why:
1. I was taken to too many games by my parents when I was growing up.
2. The games are always played when I want to do something else.
3. Every time I go to a game, somebody asks for money.
4. Although I go to games quite often, few people are friendly enough to speak to me.
5. The seats are too hard and uncomfortable. Besides, I often have to sit down front on the fifty yard line.
6. I suspect there are hypocrites sitting nearby. They come to see their friends and to look at what others are wearing rather than to see the game.
7. The field judge says things I don't agree with.
8. The band usually plays some numbers I've never heard before.
9. Some games last too long, making me get home late.
10. I have a good book on football. I can stay home and read that.

Well, there they are—ten reasons why I will never attend another football game. Kind of foolish, isn't it, to miss the joy of football for reasons like these? I wonder how many of us are missing the joys of worship, Bible study, training, and prayer for reasons just as foolish?

## 12. WHY PEOPLE GO TO CHURCH

An unknown writer offered the following analysis of why some people attend church:

> *Some go to church to take a walk;*
> *Some go there to laugh and talk.*
> *Some go there to meet a friend;*
> *Some go there their time to spend.*
> *Some go there to meet a lover;*
> *Some go there a fault to cover.*
> *Some go there for speculation;*
> *Some go there for observation.*
> *Some go there to doze and nod:*
> *The wise go there to worship God.*

## 13. LET'S GO TO CHURCH SUNDAY NIGHT

Let's go to church Sunday night. You used to, before the days when worldly attractions became so strong. Are you willing to sacrifice the value of Sunday evening church activities and of your own influence on others for a television program? If so, your Christianity has lost something.

Let's go to church Sunday night. You used to, before you acquired that circle of unchurched friends who have had more influence on you than you have on them. Surely you aren't willing to sacrifice the influence of Sunday night church services for a little social circle that is unwilling to use six other nights for its fellowship!

Let's go to church Sunday night. You used to, when friendships based on the common lordship of Christ were the friendships dearest to you. Would it be right if we turned out the lights and joined the host of other churches that have found it necessary to cut the Lord's Day in half?

Let's go to church Sunday night. Our fathers did, when services began at lamplighting time. Their religious devotion helped make our country what it is today. Is your faith as strong as theirs? Will it be in the future? What about the world in which your children will live?

## 14. CHURCH CALLED OFF BECAUSE OF RAIN

*No dashing rain can make us stay*
*When we have tickets for a play;*
*But if a drop the walk besmirch,*
*It is too wet to go to church!*

## 15. THE CITY CHURCH

*God bless the church on the Avenue*
*That hears the city's cry;*
*The church that sows the seed of the Word*
*Where the masses of men go by.*

*A church that makes, in the traffic's roar,*
*A place for an altar of prayer;*
*With a heart for the rich and a heart for the poor,*
*And looks for the burden to share.*

*A church that is true to the call of the Christ*
*Who wept for the city's need;*
*Who sent His disciples to labor for Him*
*Where the forces of evil breed.*

*A church that gives and a church that lives*
*As seen by the Master's eye;*
*God bless the church on the Avenue*
*That answers the city's cry.*

## 16. HOW TO KILL A CHURCH

1. Talk about your pastor in a critical manner. Repeat it often to others.

2. Make no preparation for your church responsibilities. Don't study your lesson or give any time to your duties as a committee member.
3. When you teach, tell your class how disappointed you are with their attendance and with what they're doing. Keep them discouraged.
4. Don't visit. This is what the church staff is hired to do.
5. Don't give. What does the church need money for, anyway?
6. Go other places on Sunday. Go anywhere but to church.
7. Show disrespect for church property. Leave the church building dirty and untidy. Drive nails in the wall and write in the hymnals.
8. Refuse to take a job in the church. Think how little time you have for yourself.
9. When you go to Sunday school, be sure to leave before the worship hour. Make this a habit.
10. No matter what proposal comes before the church, object to it! There certainly must be something wrong with it. Keep looking until you find it.

## 17. THE MISSING LAMPS

In a certain mountain village in Europe several centuries ago, a nobleman wondered what legacy he should leave to his townspeople. At last he decided to build them a church.

No one saw the complete plans for the church until it was finished. When the people gathered, they marveled at its beauty and completeness. Then someone asked, "But where are the lamps? How will it be lighted?"

The nobleman pointed to some brackets in the walls. Then he gave to each family a lamp which they were to bring with them each time they came to worship.

"Each time you are here the area where you are seated will be lighted," the nobleman said. "Each time you are not here, that area will be dark. This is to remind you that whenever you fail to come to church, some part of God's house will be dark."

## 18. SOME THOUGHTS ON CHURCH LOYALTY

Fill your place; nobody else can.

Always do your best; sing, pray, and give.

Invite your neighbor to sing; two can praise God better than one.
Think holy things; your work will go more easily tomorrow.

Help the weak in faith; this is the command of Christ.

Find the discouraged; he needs you.

Unite in every reasonable effort; you count one.

Lift up the hands of your pastor; his helpfulness will be multiplied.
Next to you may be a stranger; find him.

Engage in every part of the service; you will get more out of it.
Sing in your soul as vigorously as with your lips; this is worship.
Smile and you will make others glad.

## 19. ARE YOU BUSY ENOUGH FOR GOD TO USE?

God never goes to the lazy or the idle when He needs people for His service. When He has work to be done, He goes to those who are already at work. When God wants a great servant, He calls a busy person. Think about the great men of the Bible who were busy when God called:
   **Moses** was busy with his flock at Horeb.
   **Gideon** was busy threshing wheat by the wine press.
   **Saul** was busy searching for his father's lost sheep.
   **David** was busy caring for his father's sheep.
   **Elisha** was busy plowing with twelve yoke of oxen.
   **Nehemiah** was busy as the king's cupbearer.

**Amos** was busy following the flock.
**James** and **John** were busy mending their fishing nets.
**Matthew** was busy collecting customs.
**Saul** was busy persecuting the friends of Jesus.
Are you busy enough for God to use?

## 20. EIGHT REASONS WHY
## I ATTEND PRAYER MEETING

1. Because the church is no stronger than its prayer meeting.
2. Because of my influence upon other people.
3. Because I do not want to be a burden to my pastor.
4. Because I want to live so unsaved people will have faith in me.
5. Because I am not ashamed of the religion of Jesus Christ.
6. Because prayer meeting is the hub around which the spiritual wheel of the church revolves.
7. Because I want to live my faith before others.
8. Because when I neglect prayer meeting in my church, I harm its good name, lessen its power, and discourage its members.

## 21. THE REAL MEANING OF REDEDICATION

A young man went forward weeping when the invitation was given. He told the pastor that he wanted to rededicate his life. In the congregation that day:

A **businessman** wondered, "Will he now give me an honest day's work?"

A **teacher** mused, "Will he now apply himself and quit idling away his talents?"

A **young girl** asked herself, "On our dates will he now behave as a Christian should?"

A **mother** thought, "Sure hope this will affect the way he acts at home!"

A **Sunday school teacher** sighed, "Will he stop telling dirty jokes and making off-color remarks now?"

Unless the young man's life soon began to answer such questions with a resounding yes, he was kidding himself. He did not really rededicate his life to God.

Cheap rededications are dangerous. Weeping one's way down the aisle can be the beginning of a deeper loyalty to God, or it can be a poor substitute for forsaking sin.

If you need to return to God, do so at the first opportunity. Then pray as you go forward that rededication will begin, not end, with your public decision.

## 22. SOME SOBERING QUESTIONS FOR CHURCH MEMBERS

Suppose you had to run for church membership as a candidate runs for a political office. Would you win or lose?

Suppose your membership was good for only one year and that your reelection depended upon the good you had done in the church during that time. Would you be reelected?

Suppose your name would be dropped from membership if you didn't win to Christ at least one person a year. How long would you remain a member?

Suppose you were asked to explain just why your church should keep your name on the roll. Do you have a record of helpful service to offer in your defense?

Suppose every member of the church did as much work for the church as you are presently doing. Would more seats be needed, or would the doors of the church be closed?

Suppose you were arrested for being a Christian. Would there be enough evidence to convict you?

## 23. WHAT CHURCH MEMBERSHIP MEANS

It means coming in from the lake to attend Sunday school and worship services.

It means giving your tithe and offerings to support the church.

It means coming back to church on Sunday night.

It means taking a job somewhere in the church and doing it well.

It means helping the church fulfill its witnessing mission.

It means keeping the fellowship unbroken, loving, and forgiving.

It means praying each day for the Holy Spirit to guide and empower the church.

## 24. WHAT MY ABSENCE FROM CHURCH DID

It caused some people to question the reality of my faith.

It made some think that I was a pretender.

It made many think that I consider my spiritual welfare and that of others a matter of small concern.

It weakened the effect of the church service.

It made it harder for the preacher to preach.

It discouraged other church members and robbed them of a blessing.

It caused others to stay away from church.

It made it harder for me to resist the temptation of the devil.

It gave the devil more power and influence over lost people.

It encouraged me to become irregular in church attendance.

## 25. WHAT MY PRESENCE AT CHURCH DID

It caused people to have confidence in me.

It made people realize that I regard my spiritual welfare and that of others, matters of great importance.

It had a good effect on the services.

It made my friends feel more welcome.

It encouraged other church members and helped the pastor in his work.

It caused others to come to Christ.

It made my life stronger for another week.

It removed stumbling blocks from the sinner's path.

It pleased God.

It caused others to say, "He practices what he preaches."

## 26. THE PARABLE OF THE CHURCH THAT DIED

There was a man who lived during the twentieth century. He had a new house. Two cars and a bright, shiny boat filled his garage. A color television gleamed in his den. His family was healthy.

His custom—when he was in town, when the fish were not biting, when he was not on the beach or at the lake, when he had no guests, when he could get up on time, when he was not too tired, or when he had nothing else to do—was to go to church. When he went, he spent his time deploring the decaying state of the church: Sunday school attendance was low, the choir scanty, the congregation small, the offering poor, and the preacher discouraged. "They ought to do better," he said. "What do they think religion is all about, anyway?"

Many vacations and days off came and went. According to the way of the world, this man's children grew up. They did not go to church. The reason, their father said, was that those people down at the church had not kindled his children's interest in religion. The man's health failed. One day he noticed something strange. Those people down at the church no longer came by. He was in the hospital and they did not visit him. And lo, he was very angry!

But being a greathearted man, he decided to forgive them and go to church once more. But behold, when he arrived at the church, there was no church. There was only a corner grocery store.

"Where is the church?" he demanded.

"Oh," somebody said, "that church went out of business several years ago."

"Oh," he cried, "they should never have let it die!"

## 27. I HELPED MY CHURCH

I helped my church. I was there. I knew the pastor would be there, so I was there. My presence helped. I was one more. That cheered the pastor and gave him spiritual strength.

I helped my church. I paid my way. I did not let others pay my way any more than I permit them to buy my clothes or feed my children. I pay my household bills. I pay my way at church too. A manly, ample, competent sum must be my investment in my church.

I helped my church. I prayed for my church. I never have wanted much for myself—except strength—but I want all the blessings and power possible for my church. I pray for it as naturally as I do for my dearest loved ones. To forget my church would be to forget everything lovely. I helped my church by praying for it.

I helped my church. I was the hand and voice of my church in the homes of those who had forgotten or neglected the most important thing on earth. I went to them not with a brilliant sermon or convincing argument but with love and compassion. I witnessed for my Lord. I went as a friend to friends and found the door already open for me. I not only helped a home that needed God and the church, but I helped myself. What a joy to serve God through my church!

## 28. WHAT TO BRING TO CHURCH

Bring a holy reverence for both God and His house, the church.

Bring an unselfish spirit and an abiding love for your fellow man.

Bring your tithes and offerings.

Bring a friendly smile and a hearty handshake for friends and strangers alike.

Bring a kind word for your church, its program and leadership.

Bring a willingness to join in the worship service by singing from your heart.

Bring your visiting friends and relatives.

Bring a prayerful heart and a mind open to the Word of God.

Bring an unsaved friend and pray for him during the service.

Bring a willingness to serve the Lord in the church.

## 29. I AM YOUR CHURCH OFFICE

I am your church office. Sometimes I feel neglected. When you are planning to move, you notify every magazine to which you subscribe and you notify your friends; but sometimes you fail to notify me.

When your class plans a meeting, you notify all the members but sometimes fail to notify me. This can be embarrassing for all of us, especially when I have promised to another church group a room that you planned to use.

When a member of your family is ill, you seem to call all your friends but me. I like to know about all our people who are sick. This makes it easier for the pastor and others who want to visit in the hospitals.

So why don't you call me? Sometimes I feel neglected.

## 30. HOW TO BUILD A GREAT CHURCH

It takes very little planning to wreck a building or a business, but it takes skillful planning and diligent work to build.

It is easy to kill a church, but it takes thought and persistence to build a great church. The great churches of our land did not just happen. They have been built through persistent effort. Here are a few suggestions for building a great church:

1. Never allow a day to pass without taking time to pray for your church and its ministry.
2. Never speak to anyone without praising your church and pastor. The criticism will be spoken loud and often; see that the praise is louder.
3. Never fail to be friendly to anyone in all church services, especially to newcomers and absentees. Nothing in the world can substitute for old-fashioned friendliness.
4. Never make your church of less importance than social engagements, secular meetings, or anything else. There is no greater power for a church than that of members who quietly but emphatically put it first.
5. Never refuse an opportunity to serve. Be willing to serve anywhere you are asked. All service ranks the same with God.
6. Attend church every Sunday.

## 31. GOD BUILDS NO CHURCHES

*God builds no churches. By His plan*
*That labor has been left to man.*
*No spires miraculously arise;*
*No little mission from the skies*
*Falls in bleak and barren place*
*To be a source of strength and grace.*
*The humblest church demands its price*
*In human toil and sacrifice.*

*Men call the church the house of God*
*Toward which the toil-stained pilgrims trod*
*In search of strength and rest and hope,*
*As blindly through life's mists they grope.*
*And there God dwells, but it is man*
*Who builds that house and draws the plan;*
*Pays for mortar and the stone*
*That none need seek for God alone.*

*The humblest spire in mortal ken*
*Where God abides was built by men.*
*And if the church is still to grow,*
*Is still the light of hope to throw*
*Across the valley of despair,*
*Men still must build God's house of prayer.*
*God sends no churches from the skies;*
*Out of our hearts they must arise.*

—Edgar A. Guest

## 32. SOME STRANGE PEOPLE I KNOW

People who talk about prayer but never pray.

People who say tithing is right but never tithe.

People who want to belong to the church but never attend.

People who say the Bible is God's Word to man but never read it.

People who criticize others for things they do themselves.

People who stay away from church for trivial reasons and then sing, "Oh, How I Love Jesus."

People who continue in sin all their lives but expect to go to heaven.

## 33. IS YOUR CHRISTIANITY FIRST CLASS?

Christianity is the greatest thing in the world, yet so many church members live and act as though being a Christian is second rate.

Do you raise the quality of your church by the way you participate in its worship services, its Wednesday night services, the Sunday school and training programs, the mission program, the financial program, and the witnessing program?

How much difference would it make if you came to worship services each Lord's Day saying to yourself, "This hour is going to be one of the real highlights of my life this week."

Or suppose you didn't seek a bargain-basement stewardship, but gave freely and joyously of your time, ability, and money? What a difference this would make!

Is Christianity the greatest thing in the world to you, or are you giving God second place in your life?

## 34. SERVE CHRIST THROUGH YOUR CHURCH

Some people ask, "Can I be a Christian without working in the church?" The answer is yes. But let's put this question in perspective. Being a Christian without serving in the church is something like:
A **student** who will not go to school.
A **soldier** who will not join an army.
A **citizen** who does not vote or pay his taxes.
A **salesman** with no customers.
An **explorer** with no base camp.
A **seaman** on a ship without a crew.
A **businessman** on a desert island.
An **author** without readers.
A **tuba player** without a band.
A **parent** without a family.
A **football player** without a team.
A **politician** who refuses to meet people.
A **scientist** who refuses to share his findings with others.

## 35. A CHURCH GARDEN

First, plant five rows of peas:
    Presence.
    Promptness.
    Preparation.
    Purity.
    Perseverance.
Next to these plant three rows of squash:
    Squash gossip.
    Squash criticism.
    Squash indifference.

No garden is complete without turnips:

Turn up for the meetings.

Turn up with a smile.

Turn up with new ideas.

Turn up with determination to make everything count for something good and worthwhile.

## 36. I AM YOUR CHURCH

I am your church. I am here because you built me. I am beautifully situated in your midst. In the center of your community I will be a cherished landmark to the thousands who come to my door over the years. You built me because you knew that your life would be incomplete and unfulfilled without me.

I am your church. I am here not simply to adorn, but to serve. Your children and youth come to me to learn the ways of honesty, industry, morality, and religion. Your brides and grooms come to my altar that their weddings may be hallowed and sweetened by divine blessings.

I am your church. I comfort your sick and sorrowing. I bury your dead and offer rest and solace to the weary. I bring pardon and peace to those who are burdened with sin. My message of mercy brings new life.

I am your church. My doors are open to all—rich or poor, bond or free. My pulpit rings out the message of good will to men, of peace and pardon, and of a Savior's love to all. I teach you the way of life and guide you on the road to heaven.

I am your church. Come and worship with me; support me; and I will serve you all your days on this earth and beyond.

## 37. ETIQUETTE FOR CHURCH MEMBERS

1. Arrive early. You need at least five minutes to settle your mind before the service begins.

2. Do not whisper, read, or do anything during the services that would destroy the reverence of worship.
3. Never walk down the aisle when Scripture is being read, prayer offered, or a special song sung.
4. Sit near the front if you are on time. Occupy the center of the pew so there will be as little disturbance as possible when late comers are seated.
5. If you are late, take a seat near the door.
6. Sing if you can; share your hymnal with strangers.
7. Do promptly whatever is asked of the congregation.
8. Be as courteous to guests in your church as you would in your home, welcoming everyone warmly. Introduce strangers to the pastor. Never pass anyone in the Lord's house without speaking to them. Make your church a friendly place.

## 38. THE SIN OF INDIFFERENCE

What word comes to your mind first when you hear the word *love?* Most of us think of opposites and would have to say *hate*. But hate is not the opposite of love. The opposite of love is indifference.

When a husband or wife says "I hate you," the case is not hopeless. That home can be saved. But when a husband or wife becomes totally indifferent to the other, that home is in real jeopardy.

Nothing hurts our Lord more than indifference. He prefers being hated to being ignored. I wonder how Jesus feels about those who are indifferent and apathetic toward their church?

## 39. A FRUSTRATING EXPERIENCE IN CHURCH

It had been a hard week. I came to church to renew my spiritual strength and to wait on the Lord for His message. I needed strength and encouragement. I thought I would find these in worship, in the presence of the Lord in His house.

People entered the church all around me with friendly greetings. Soon these greetings grew into a noisy hum as the auditorium began to fill. The buzz continued, even after the organ prelude began. The choir filed in, and the pastor took his place. The congregation stood up for the opening hymn and the invocation. The constant buzzing continued as the pastor read from God's Word.

After the sermon the invitation hymn was announced and the people stood to sing. I was puzzled and confused to see so many members leaving during this most important part of the service.

When it was over, I left God's house frustrated and disturbed rather than refreshed and strengthened.

## 40. I DID NOT STAY FOR WORSHIP SERVICES

I came to Sunday school today, but I did not stay for worship services. By so doing:

I told my church I do not need it; I received all the spiritual power I needed during Sunday school.

I told the children in Sunday school it is not necessary for them to stay for church in order to be the right kind of church member.

I told the stranger passing by the church door that we do not like our worship program or our pastor's preaching.

I told my unsaved friend that I am not interested in helping him find Christ as his Savior. I realize that unless he is saved in the church, he will probably not be saved at all, but that is no real concern of mine.

I told God that I had seen enough of Him today. I do not care to sing praises to His name. I do not care to hear His Word read any more. I do not want to bow my knee to Him and worship.

## 41. A HALF-HEARTED PRAYER

*I love Thy church, O God;*
*Her walls before me stand:*

*But please excuse my absence, Lord;*
*This bed is simply grand!*

*A charge to keep I have;*
*A God to glorify;*
*But, Lord, no cash from me:*
*Thy glory comes too high.*

*Am I a soldier of the cross,*
*A follower of the Lamb?*
*Yes! Though I seldom pray or pay,*
*I still insist I am.*

*Must Jesus bear the cross alone,*
*And all the world go free?*
*No! Others, Lord, should do their part,*
*But please don't count on me.*

*Praise God from whom all blessings flow;*
*Praise Him, all creatures here below!*
*Oh, loud my hymns of praise I bring*
*Because it doesn't cost to sing!*

## 42. A MESSAGE FOR INACTIVE CHURCH MEMBERS

We've been missing you at church recently. It's been several weeks since we've seen any of you at Sunday school or worship services. Before you drop out completely from church life, consider several things about your inactivity:

1. Consider your Lord's will. Does He want you inactive?
2. Consider your children. It doesn't take many years of inactivity on your part to guarantee that they will grow up without knowing Christ. Do you want that?
3. Consider your life. Have you noticed the un-Christian actions and thoughts increasing in your life? Do you remember when you committed your life to Christ?
4. Consider your world and talk a lot about the bad shape it is in. As an inactive church member, are you helping or hurting?

It's true that church attendance is not all there is to being a Christian, but it certainly is vital. Without it, the rest of life suffers. Don't remain inactive. Great joy awaits you when you return to active service and participation in your church.

## 43. WHAT THE CHURCH IS TO ME

A door:
> Into an opportunity for service.
> Into the most useful life.
> Into the best of life's experiences.
> Into the most hopeful future.

An armory:
> To get power to fight evil.
> To get inspiration to keep doing right.
> To get an uplifting influence.
> To learn how to use spiritual weapons.
> To get a vision of Christ.

An anchor:
> To steady me in the storm.
> To keep me from the breakers.
> To guide me in the strenuous life.
> To hold me lest I drift from God.
> To save me in the hour of temptation.

## 44. ARE YOU A GUEST CHRISTIAN?

A guest Christian waits until other people have done all the work, then steps in to enjoy the blessings of their labor. He receives while others give. Others may serve the Lord with gladness; others may pay the church's bills; others may sacrifice to worship each week; but guest Christians congratulate themselves on getting by without doing any of this work themselves. They are guests who enjoy the fruits and labor of others.

People who depend on the church for the religious and moral instruction of their children should support the church by their presence as well as their means. Otherwise they become guests, enjoying what others provide but failing to help in any way themselves. Guest Christians attend church only on special occasions and contribute only when special services are rendered. The rest of the time they receive the benefits of the church without supporting it in any way.

"Follow me" calls for active discipleship, but many people want the blessings of discipleship without the cost. Jesus calls for workers, not guests.

## 45. THE DEVIL'S ADVOCATES

One of the most foolish things a warrior can do is go to battle without first knowing his enemy. Satan has planted many of his best agents among us. Let's expose a few of them:

First is **Chronic Complainer**. He is silent only when the church is idle.

His able lieutenant is **Ever Offended**. Disagree with him and he'll take his toys and go home.

Their capable assistant is **Avid Advisor**. No matter how hard you try or how well you do, he will always tell you how you could have done it better.

Then there is **Church Jumper**. He is always sure that somewhere is a perfect church where everyone and everything is in complete harmony. If he finds a church like that, let's hope he doesn't join it; he might spoil it!

## 46. THE PERFECT CHURCH

*I think that I shall never see
A church that's all it ought to be:
A church whose members never stray
Beyond the straight and narrow way.*

*A church that has no empty pews;
Whose pastor never has the blues;
A church whose deacons always deak,
And none are proud, and all are meek.*

*Where gossips never peddle lies
Or make complaints or criticize.*

*Where all are always sweet and kind*
*And all to others' faults are blind.*

*Such perfect churches there may be,*
*But none of them is known to me;*
*But still I'll work and pray and plan*
*To make our church the best I can.*

## 47. SOME MISTAKES PARENTS CAN MAKE

Thinking that three hours at the movies are harmless for your child but that two hours of church and Sunday school are too much for his nervous system.

Giving your child a nickel for the offering and fifty cents for the movies.

Letting your child listen to several hours of radio and television thrillers a day and allowing no time for a short prayer and a few Bible verses.

Making sure that your child learns his weekday lessons and not caring if he knows his Sunday school lesson.

Letting your child decide for himself whether to go to church.

## 48. LOST IN THE "WOULDS"

Some church members are hopelessly lost in the "woulds":

I would go to Sunday school today, but I enjoy too much my little extra sleep on Sunday morning.

I would take my children to Sunday school and church, but Sunday is my only day to play golf.

I would teach a Sunday school class, but my job just doesn't leave time for that much involvement in church.

I would witness to others about Christ, but I never seem to say the right words.

I would give more to the church, but there's just not much left after paying the bills.

The only way to find your way out of the "woulds" is to set your eyes upon Christ. He will show the way.

## 49. ARE YOU IN ONE OF THESE GROUPS?

Of all the people who belong to our churches today:

Ten percent cannot be found.

Twenty percent never pray.

Thirty percent never read the Bible.

Forty percent never give anything to the church.

Fifty percent seldom attend services.

Sixty percent never give to missions.

Seventy-five percent serve nowhere in the church.

Eighty-five percent never go to midweek prayer services.

Ninety percent never have family worship.

Ninety-five percent have never told another person about Christ.

## 50. DON'T STAY AWAY FROM CHURCH

Don't stay away from church:

Because you are poor. There is no admission charge.

Because it rains. Most of us go to work in the rain.

Because it's hot. It's sometimes hot at your house too.

Because no one invited you. People go many other places without being asked.

Because you have little children. We have a well-supervised nursery and other facilities for children.

Because you don't like the pastor. He's human just as you are.

Because there are hypocrites at church. You associate with hypocrites every day.

Because you have guests in your home. They will admire your loyalty if you bring them along.

Because you need a little weekend vacation occasionally. No one can take a vacation from God.

Because your clothes are not expensive. Our church is not a fashion show.

Because our church standards are too high. Are they any higher than the Biblical standards for a church?

# 2
# Sunday School Attendance and Support

---

## 51. HOW SUNDAY SCHOOLS GROW

In his book on the one hundred largest Sunday schools in the United States, Dr. Elmer Towns listed eight characteristics that made these churches and their Sunday school programs outstanding:

1. Their members are unapologetically committed to reaching people for Jesus Christ.
2. They accept the doctrines of the infallibility of the Bible and the absolute lordship of Jesus Christ.
3. They consider Sunday school a must for all age levels, and they require visitation.
4. Their worship services are spontaneous and warmhearted, and they place great emphasis on heartfelt singing, preaching, and praying.
5. They are really excited about what God is doing in their churches. They talk about their churches constantly and in a positive way.
6. They financially support their churches willingly and freely.

7. They are convinced that Jesus is coming again and that the time to reach lost people is short.
8. They believe in their churches and support all activities faithfully.

## 52. FOURTEEN WAYS TO KILL A SUNDAY SCHOOL

1. Attend only when convenient.
2. When you do attend, arrive late.
3. Grumble about having to attend.
4. Criticize the officers and teachers in front of your family and friends.
5. Refuse to accept any responsibility in the Sunday school. If you ever do accept any, do it grudgingly and neglect it often.
6. Never study your lesson.
7. Always show your lack of interest in the lesson.
8. Appear relieved when the class is over. Act as if you've wasted your time.
9. Refuse to welcome visitors; make them feel that you belong and they don't.
10. Criticize every new idea that's suggested.
11. Dominate discussions; always insist that your opinion is right.
12. Regard the teachers of your children as upstarts and busybodies.
13. Show your distrust or disapproval of teachers when they call in your home.
14. Never sacrifice for the Sunday school; leave that to somebody else.

## 53. A SPECIAL WORD
## FOR SUNDAY SCHOOL TEACHERS

1. Our teachers must attend. Absentee teachers teach a lot; they teach that Sunday school is a casual thing not to be taken seriously. To be absent four or five times a year is understandable, but to be absent ten or fifteen times devastates a class. You must teach your class Sunday after Sunday

until the members realize that you consider Sunday school important and that you love and care for them.

2. Our teachers must be on time. Teachers in public schools are required to arrive before the students do. The Sunday school teacher simply must do the same. This is another way to tell the class that Sunday school is important.

3. Our teachers must be prepared. Nothing will turn off a class quicker than a poorly prepared teacher. You simply cannot become a good teacher without spending plenty of time in study and prayer.

4. Our teachers must visit. To get to know your class members is the first task of a Christian teacher. You must visit them to find out who they are and what they are like. Visitation helps build up the class. A good teacher ought to have more members in his class at the end of the year than when the year started.

## 54. A TEACHER'S CODE OF ETHICS

As a teacher in my church, I will do my best:

To come before my class each Sunday with a prepared heart and a prepared attitude.

To make every effort to grow in the grace and knowledge of the Lord Jesus Christ and to help my pupils do the same.

To contact absentees promptly, personally, and persistently.

To set an example in faithfulness, regular attendance, punctuality, and stewardship.

To make my instruction personal and practical, adapting the lesson to the needs and interests of my class.

To try conscientiously to win every class member to Christ and to help him live a Christian life.

To be loyal to my church and Sunday school.

To cooperate gladly with my pastor, Sunday school director, and other officers.

To study diligently and use every possible means to improve my teaching.

To esteem Christ first, others second, and myself last.

## 55. OUR SUNDAY SCHOOL PLATFORM

The Sunday school is:
> The friend of childhood.
> The inspiration of youth.
> The strength of middle life.
> The comfort of declining years.

The Sunday school has:
> God's day for its time.
> God's house for its place.
> God's book for its text.

The Sunday school deserves:
> The full support,
> The prayerful interest,
> The loyal cooperation,
> of every member of the church.

## 56. THE CLASS MEMBER'S RESPONSIBILITY IN SUNDAY SCHOOL

1. Study your lesson. So many times we get nothing out of the lesson because we haven't prepared. If Sunday school is to be a learning experience, we must prepare. We ought to take Sunday school as seriously as our other educational opportunities.
2. Attend regularly. If some people attended school as they attend Sunday school, they would almost certainly fail.
3. If you know more than the teacher, perhaps you should consider teaching a class yourself. Good students of the Bible are hard to find. It's even harder to get them to accept a teaching position.
4. Invite people whom you know to attend Sunday school with you. Every business, institution, and activity must

have advertising and public relations people. We do a pretty poor job of informing the public of our product. When was the last time you visited a prospect, challenged an absentee to get back in the swing of attendance, or gave someone a ride to Sunday school?

## 57. THE TEACHER'S RESPONSIBILITY IN SUNDAY SCHOOL

1. Know each person individually—his home, school, friends, habits, and needs. Vistation helps you do this.
2. Know the truth you are trying to help pupils understand and accept. What does the Bible say about it? How does it relate to the lives of your class members? Attending regular meetings of the Sunday school teachers and officers helps you learn how to do this.
3. Live up to what you profess. Teach by example. Regular church attendance is a good place to start.
4. Be available when someone needs to talk. Listen without criticizing, without showing alarm or amusement at the problem, and without alienating the person. A good prayer time helps you recall the needs of your class members.

## 58. THE TEACHER'S PSALM

The Lord is my helper; I shall not fear in guiding these pupils.

He leadeth me to the heart of the truth and prepareth the mind of the pupils for the truth.

He giveth me a vision of the immortality of these lives.

He leadeth me to see the sacredness of teaching His Book.

Yea, though I become discouraged and despair at times, yet shall I lift my head, for His promises cannot fail me.

His word will not return to Him void, and my faith undimmed shall burn through all the coming years.

Thou walkest before me that the seed planted shall grow.

Thou shalt stand by my side on Sunday and speak through these lips so that these pupils may feel the nearness of God.

Thou shalt cause each broken effort to gather sheaves through unnumbered years. My joy is full when I know that every effort in Thy name shall abide forever.

Surely Thy love and watchcare shall be with me every day of my life, and some day I shall live with those who turn many to righteousness for ever and ever.

*—Rosalee Mills Appleby*

# 3
# Visitation, Witnessing, and Christian Outreach

---

## 59. SOME REASONS WHY I VISIT

I visit because it was the visit of someone else that started me attending church services regularly.

I visit because it was the visit of someone else that encouraged me during a very difficult time in my life.

I visit because Christ commanded me to spread His kingdom.

I visit because Jesus wants me to, and I want to please Him.

I visit because my Christian experience needs an outlet. I want to give as well as receive.

I visit because of the blessings I receive when calling on other people.

I visit because people need help. I can't do a lot, but God will use me to bless other people.

I visit because people are lost without Christ. I don't know much theology, but I can share what Christ has done for me.

I visit because people need to study the Bible and worship regularly, and personal visitation is the best way to get them to do this.

## 60. PERSONAL VISITATION WILL DO THE JOB

Would you like to grow spiritually? Visitation will do the job.

Do you want to see our church program grow and prosper? Visitation will do the job.

Do you want to see lost people won to Christ? Visitation will do the job.

Would you like to see unaffiliated and unconcerned church members become active members? Visitation will do the job.

Would you like to follow the command of Christ in Acts 1:8? Visitation will do the job.

Personal visitation is the answer. How much have you been doing?

## 61. KEEP ON GOING

*One step won't take you very far;*
*You've got to keep on walking.*
*One word won't tell people who you are;*
*You've got to keep on talking.*
*One inch won't make you very tall;*
*You've got to keep on growing.*
*One little call won't do it all;*
*You've got to keep on going.*

## 62. GOING BACK DOES IT

How many times should we visit a prospect for the church? Perhaps the business world will give us a clue. Successful salesmen are those who keep going back, as the following statistics demonstrate:

Forty-eight percent of the salesmen quit after only one call.

Twenty-five percent quit after two.

Fifteen percent quit after three.

The remaining twelve percent keep on calling, and these do eighty percent of the business.

Should not Christians go even beyond the salesmen of the business world? The way to build a great church is: Visit! Visit! Visit!

## 63. HOW TO BECOME A CHRISTIAN WITNESS

If you really want to become a witness for Christ, here are some things you can do:

1. Pray for personal victory in the Christian life. If you are defeated personally, you can never become a dynamic witness for Christ.
2. Pray for lost people in particular. There may be some among your loved ones. There most surely are some among your friends and acquaintances. Pray for them by name. Put them on a prayer list and keep them on your mind and heart.
3. Pray for divine direction. Pray that God will lead you to someone who needs Christ and that He will help you say just the right word. The Holy Spirit can guide you in both areas.
4. Pray for the pastor and the church services every time the church meets. While the pastor is preaching, pray for him. If possible, be in the worship services yourself and render a silent witness.

## 64. WHAT OUTREACH AND WITNESSING WILL DO FOR A CHURCH

Outreach and Christian witnessing will do a number of things for a church:

It will kill petty bickering, criticism, and complaining. People who are busy witnessing for Christ don't have time for petty, trivial things.

It will revive the church. Only in the spirit of consecration and prayer can a church witness for Christ. When these twin graces are practiced, the things which displease the Lord will be removed.

It will encourage unaffiliated church members to move their membership. For every person who makes a profession of faith during a worship service, usually two others will transfer their membership to the church.

It will kindle a kindred spirit in other church members. When we see a fellow church member witnessing for Christ, we ask, "Why can't I do that?"

A church can never achieve true greatness until it becomes a witnessing and winning church.

## 65. SATAN'S SUBVERSION OF THE GREAT COMMISSION

The New Testament program for the church is the Great Commission. The church which follows it will be a mighty redemptive instrument in the hands of God. Since Satan knows this better than we do, he has always tried to subvert the Great Commission. He does not deny its validity openly, but he seeks to distort and misrepresent it. He does this in five ways:

1. He substitutes the good for the best. He causes us to substitute attending, singing, giving, and even praying for going. He is willing for us to be busy about many good things if we will forget the best—telling others about Jesus.
2. He reduces its requirements. There are four requirements in the Commission—going, winning, baptizing, and training. When Satan gets us to emphasize going to the neglect of baptizing those won and teaching them to win others, he wins a great victory.
3. He limits its scope. The scope of the Great Commission is

worldwide. He fights to get us to neglect the world for our Jerusalem or to neglect personal witnessing for our collective mission task.

4. He misrepresents the nature of Christian witness. Witnessing is twofold—by life and by lip. It is not one or the other but both. The person who says "I don't talk to people about Christ, but I witness with my life" is deceived.

5. He professionalizes the Great Commission. Satan has convinced many of us that the task of evangelism belongs to professionals—pastors and other church staff members. Since the church is made up mainly of laymen, this excuses most Christians from the important task of the Great Commission.

Has Satan pulled one of these tricks on you? He has been successful with multitudes of people and churches. So beware.

## 66. THE CHALLENGE OF OUTREACH

Go:

Out from the warmth and joy of fellowship in your church.

Out because Christ commanded us to go.

Out because we as Christians are His ambassadors.

Out in obedience because we love Christ.

Out because we care for the lost.

Out to those who do not know Christ as Savior.

Into the highways and hedges:

Where a baby is born every two seconds.

Where parental and juvenile delinquency are rampant.

Where an immigrant crosses our borders every two minutes.

Where life's highways lead to school, office, shop, or store.

Where people are groping for meaning in life.

That:

The seeker may find truth.

The sorrowing may find comfort.

The weary may find rest.

The troubled may find peace.

The sinner may find eternal life.

## 67. THE MAN BY THE ROAD

*If I were the man by the side of the road*
  *Who watches the world go by,*
*I'd stop every man with a frown on his face*
  *And ask him the reason why.*

*I'd stop everyone with sad, weary eyes*
  *And find out what made him so;*
*I'd point out to each the Christ on the cross*
  *And help him His love to know.*

*I do not live by the side of the road*
  *Where the race of man passes on;*
*But I meet them each day on the path of life—*
  *Those wanderers far from home.*

*You don't have to live in a house by the road*
  *To scatter the sunshine of love;*
*But wherever you live, if a man asks the way,*
  *Just point him to heaven above.*

## 68. SOME SHOCKING STATISTICS

Here are some statistics that emphasize the urgency of witnessing for Christ today:

1. There are 138,000 more lost people in the world this morning than there were yesterday morning.
2. When you arrive at your Sunday school class next Sunday, there will be about 1,000,000 more lost people in the world than when you arrived last Sunday.
3. Each year ends with about 50,000,000 more lost people in

the world than when the year began.

4. About 146,000 people will die around the world within the next twenty-four hours. Most of them will not know Christ as Savior and Lord.

5. A line composed of all the lost people in the world would circle the earth thirty times. This line will grow at the rate of twenty miles per day.

## 69. IT BEGINS AT YOUR FRONT DOOR

It's unbelievable!

If all the unsaved people in the world were to line up single file at your front door, the line would reach around the world thirty times. And what's worse, this line would grow at the rate of twenty miles per day!

If you should drive fifty miles an hour, ten hours per day, it would take you four years and forty days to get to the end of the line, and by the time you reached it, it would have become thirty thousand miles long.

And all of this begins at your front door. Jesus said, "Ye shall be witnesses unto me both in Jerusalem, and in all Judaea, and in Samaria, and unto the uttermost part of the earth."

## 70. A VISIT

*One day I rang a doorbell*
*In a casual sort of way;*
*'Twas not a formal visit*
*And there wasn't much to say.*

*I don't remember what I said—*
*It matters not, I guess—*
*But I found a heart in hunger,*
*A soul in deep distress.*

*He said I came from heaven,*
*And I've often wondered why;*
*He said I came to see him*
*When no other help was nigh.*

*It meant so little to me*
  *To knock at a stranger's door,*
*But it meant heaven to him*
  *And God's peace forevermore.*

# 4
# Revival Support and Preparation

## 71. PRAY FOR OUR REVIVAL

The most important way each of us can prepare for the coming revival is to pray. Through prayer God speaks to us, showing us our spiritual needs and leading us into a right relationship with Him.

God then fills our hearts with concern for the spiritual welfare of others and leads us to share Christ with them. Let us then give ourselves to prayer—privately and in groups, as the Spirit leads. The more we pray in sincerity and truth, the more God will revive spiritually our church and community.

## 72. HOW TO HAVE A REVIVAL

Revival doesn't just happen. It must be planned for, worked up, and prayed down. We as Christians must be involved in it. We ought to pray as if revival depended entirely on God, and work as if it depended entirely on us.

We can have a revival if we:

    Ask God to revive us.

    Ask Him to use us in reviving others.

    Help spread news of the revival.

    Invite friends to attend the services.

    Give priority to the services in our schedules.

    Open our hearts to God's will.

    Do what God directs us to do.

    Love Jesus more than anyone or anything else.

## 73. HOW TO GET READY FOR REVIVAL

**R**ecall your own Christian experience.
enew your promises to God.
esolve to do your best in His service.

**E**nter into the revival enthusiastically.
xert every effort to win someone to Christ.
nlist this new convert in service.

**V**isualize the condition of the lost.
ow that you will do something about it.
oice your deep desire in daily prayer.

**I**nvite people to all the services.
mpress upon them the importance of attending.
ntensify your own efforts to live like a Christian.

**V**iew the fields that are "white unto harvest."
olunteer your services wherever they are needed.
isit in homes as much as possible.

**A**spire to all that is good and holy.
ttend every service if possible.
llow God to use you.

**L**ook at the needy and sinful world.
ove people freely and abundantly.
et the Holy Spirit guide you.

## 74. WHAT OTHERS HAVE DONE DURING REVIVAL

A **doctor** gave tracts, folders, and publicity about the revival to his patients.

A **dentist** made his chair a witness stand.

A **barber** witnessed to his customers and gave them Christian literature.

A **farmer** dropped his work long enough to talk to a person who needed Christ.

An **ordinary man** became "God's chauffeur" and brought lost people to the services.

A **Sunday school teacher** taught the plan of salvation, and three of her students came to know Christ.

A **housewife** talked to delivery men, repairmen, the paper boy, and several of her neighbors about Jesus and the revival.

An **insurance agent** used part of his time with prospective customers to tell them about Christ and His assurance.

You can do something too! It all depends on your willingness to be used of God.

# 5
# Inspiration
# for Daily Living

## 75. GO THROUGH THE DAY WITH GOD

*Begin the day with God;*
  *Kneel down to Him in prayer;*
*Lift up your heart to His abode*
  *And seek His love to share.*

*Open the Book of God*
  *And read a portion there,*
*That it may hallow all thy thoughts*
  *And sweeten all thy care.*

*Go through the day with God,*
  *Whate'er thy work may be;*
*Where'er thou art—at home, abroad—*
  *He still is near to thee.*

*Converse in mind with God,*
  *Thy spirit heavenward raise;*
*Acknowledge every good bestowed*
  *And offer grateful praise.*

*Conclude the day with God;*
*Thy sins to Him confess;*
*Trust in the Lord's atoning blood*
*And plead His righteousness.*

*Lie down at night with God,*
*Who gives His servants sleep;*
*And when thou tread'st the vale of death,*
*He will thee guard and keep.*

### 76. TAKE TIME

Take time:
To **think**. It is the source of power.
To **play**. It is the secret of perpetual youth.
To **read**. It is the fountain of wisdom.
To **pray**. It is the greatest power on earth.
To **love** and **be loved**. It is a God-given privilege.
To **be friendly**. It is the road to happiness.

### 77. THE REWARD OF CARRYING THE CROSS

Carry the cross patiently, and with perfect submission, and in the end it will carry you. —*Thomas a Kempis*

### 78. LORD, I CONFESS

I've been long on "oughtness" and short on "isness."

I've been long on doing and short on being.

I've been long on what I believe and short on whom I believe.

I've been long on baptism and short on forgiveness.

I've been long on the Book of God and short on following the teachings of this Book.

I've been long on law and short on love.

I've been long on judgment and short on mercy.

I've been long on meddling and short on ministry.

I've been long on methods and short on motives.

I've been long on righteous indignation and short on compassion.

I've been long on sins of the flesh and short on sins of neglect.

## 79. A SERMON THAT REALLY SPEAKS

*I'd rather see a sermon*
  *Than hear one any day;*
*I'd rather one should walk with me*
  *Than merely tell the way.*

*The eye's a better pupil*
  *And more willing than the ear;*
*Fine counsel is confusing,*
  *But example's always clear.*

*And the best of all the preachers*
  *Are the men who live their creeds;*
*For to see good put in action*
  *Is what everybody needs.*
                        —Edgar A. Guest

## 80. WHO WALKS WITH GOD

*Who walks with God must make his way*
*Across far distances and gray,*
*To goals that others do not see,*
*Where others do not care to be.*

*Who walks with God must have no fear*
*When danger and defeat appear;*
*Nor stop when hope seems all but gone,*
*For God, our God, moves ever on.*

*Who walks with God must press ahead*
*When sun or cloud is overhead;*

*When all the waiting thousands cheer*
*Or when they only stop to sneer.*

*When all the challenges leave the hours*
*And naught is left but jaded powers;*
*But he will someday reach the dawn,*
*For God, our God, moves ever on.*

## 81. A GUIDE TO GOOD LIVING

Learn to laugh; a laugh is better than medicine.

Learn to mind your own business; few men can handle their own well.

Learn to tell a story; a well-told story is like a sunbeam in a sickroom.

Learn to say kind things; nobody ever resents them.

Learn to stop grumbling; if you can't see any good in the world, keep the bad to yourself.

Learn to love other people; this is a doorway to the kingdom.

Learn to place yourself in the other person's position before condemning; it might change your whole outlook.

Learn the great lessons of the Bible; no greater lessons can be learned.

## 82. IF

*If you want to be rich—give!*
*If you want to be poor—grasp!*
*If you want to be needy—hoard!*
*If you want abundance—scatter!*

## 83. STRENGTH FOR THE ASKING

A little boy was having difficulty lifting a heavy stone. His father came along just then. Noting the boy's failure, he asked, "Are you using all your strength?"

"Yes, I am," the boy said impatiently.

"No, you're not," the father answered. "I'm right here waiting, and you haven't asked me to help you."

When we are faced with a problem that seems unsolvable or a burden that is too heavy, we might ask ourselves, "Are we using all our strength?" Our Father, too, is waiting to help.

## 84. THE MEASURE OF A MAN

*Not, How did he die?*
  *But, How did he live?*
*Not, What did he gain?*
  *But, What did he give?*

*Not, What was his station?*
  *But, Had he a heart?*
*And, How did he play*
  *His God-given part?*

## 85. I AM ONE

*I am only one,*
*But I am one;*
*I cannot do everything,*
*But I can do something.*

*What I can do,*
*I ought to do;*
*And what I ought to do,*
*By the grace of God, I will do.*

## 86. SOME THINGS I TRIED

I laughed at difficulties and found them disappearing.

I accepted heavy responsibilities and found them growing lighter.

I faced a bad situation and found it clearing up.

I told the truth and found it the easiest way out.

I did an honest day's work and found it the most rewarding.

I believed that people were honest, and I found them measuring up to my expectations.

I trusted God each day and found Him surprising me with His goodness.

## 87. THE POWER OF WORDS

*A careless word may kindle strife;*
*A cruel word may wreck a life.*
*A bitter word may hate instill;*
*A brutal word may smite and kill.*
*A gracious word may smooth the way;*
*A joyous word may light the day.*
*A timely word may lessen stress;*
*A loving word may heal and bless.*

## 88. THE STORY OF THE PRAYING HANDS

All of us have admired the art masterpiece known as "The Praying Hands." Here's the fascinating story behind that masterful work of art.

In the late fifteenth century two struggling young art students, Albrecht Dürer and Franz Knigstein, worked as laborers to earn money to continue their art studies. The work was long and hard; it left them little time to study art.

Finally they agreed to draw lots and let the loser support them both while the winner continued to study. Albrecht won. If and when he attained success, Albrecht agreed to then support Franz so that he too could finish his studies.

After Albrecht achieved success, he returned to keep his bargain with Franz. He soon discovered the enormous sacrifice his friend had made for him. As Franz had worked at hard labor, his fingers had become twisted and stiff. His long, slender fingers and sensitive hands had been ruined for life. He could no longer manage the delicate brush strokes so necessary to execute fine paintings. In spite of the price he had paid, Franz was not bitter. He was happy that his friend Albrecht had attained success.

One day Albrecht saw his loyal friend kneeling, his rough and gnarled hands entwined in silent prayer. Albrecht sketched his friend's hands. From this sketch he later completed a truly great masterpiece. He gave it the simple but moving title, "The Praying Hands."

## 89. GOD OF THE HUMDRUM

If God is not in your typewriter as well as your hymnbook, there is something wrong with your religion.

If God does not enter your kitchen, there is something wrong with your kitchen.

If you can't take God into your recreation, there is something wrong with your play.

If God for you does not smile, there is something wrong with your idea of God.

We all believe in the God of the heroic. What we need most these days is the God of the humdrum—the commonplace, the everyday.

—*Peter Marshall*

## 90. THE MAN IN THE GLASS

*When you get what you want in your struggle with life*
*And the world makes you king for a day,*
*Then go to the mirror and look at yourself*
*And see what that guy has to say.*

*For it isn't your father, or mother, or wife*
*Whose judgment upon you must pass;*

*The fellow whose verdict counts most in your life*
  *Is the man staring back from the glass.*

*He's the man to please, never mind all the rest;*
  *For he stays with you to the end;*
*And you've passed your most dangerous, difficult test*
  *If the man in the glass is your friend.*

*You may mimic Jack Horner and chisel a plum*
  *And think you're a wonderful guy;*
*But the man in the glass says you're only a bum*
  *If you can't look him straight in the eye.*

*You can fool the whole world down the pathway of years*
  *And get pats on the back as you pass;*
*But your final reward will be heartaches and tears*
  *If you've cheated the man in the glass.*

## 91. HOW TO GROW AS A CHRISTIAN

Pray without ceasing (I Thess. 5:17).
Rejoice in the Lord always (Phil. 4:4).
Add to your faith, virtue (II Peter 1:5).
Ye have not because ye ask not (James 4:2).

Whatsoever he saith unto you, do it (John 2:5).
Only fear the Lord and serve Him (I Sam. 12:24).
Remember the words of the Lord Jesus (Acts 20:35).
Keep thyself pure (I Tim. 5:22).

Go ye into all the world and preach (Mark 16:15).
In all thy ways acknowledge Him (Prov. 3:6).
Vow and pray unto the Lord your God (Ps. 76:11).
Endure hardness as a good soldier of Christ (II Tim. 2:3).

## 92. TEARING DOWN OR BUILDING?

*I watched them tearing a building down,*
*A gang of men in a busy town;*
*With a heave-ho and a lusty yell*
*They swung a beam, and the building fell.*

I asked the foreman, "Are these men skilled,
And the men you'd hire if you had to build?"
He gave a laugh and said, "No, indeed,
Just common labor is all I need;
I can easily wreck in a day or two
What builders have taken a year to do."

And I thought to myself as I went my way,
Which of these roles have I tried to play?
Am I a builder who works with care,
Measuring life by the rule and square?

Am I shaping my deeds to a well-made plan,
Patiently doing the best I can?
Or am I a wrecker who walks the town,
Content with the labor of tearing down?
—Roe Fulkerson

## 93. PRAYER

Prayer is so simple,
It is like quietly opening the door
And slipping into the very presence of God;
There in the stillness
To listen to His voice;
Perhaps to petition
Or only to listen.
It matters not;
Just to be there
In His presence
Is prayer.

## 94. A STATE OF MIND

If you think you are beaten, you are;
    If you think you dare not, you don't;
If you'd like to win but think you can't,
    It's almost a cinch you won't.

63

*If you think you'll lose, you've lost;*
*For out in the world you'll find*
*Success begins with a person's will:*
*It's all in the state of mind.*

*Life's battles don't always seem to go*
*To the strongest or fastest man,*
*But sooner or later the man who wins*
*Is the one who thinks he can.*

## 95. HOW TO TELL A WINNER FROM A LOSER

A loser says, "Nobody knows." A winner says, "Let's find out."

When a loser makes a mistake, he says, "It wasn't my fault." When a winner makes a mistake, he says, "I was wrong."

A loser tries to go around a problem and never gets past it. A winner goes through a problem.

A loser makes promises. A winner makes commitments.

A loser says, "I'm not as bad as a lot of other people." A winner says, "I'm good, but not as good as I ought to be."

A loser tries to tear down those who are superior to him. A winner tries to learn from them.

A loser says, "That's the way it's always been done here." A winner says, "There ought to be a better way to do it."

## 96. OVERCOMING FEAR THROUGH FAITH

An inscription above the fireplace of an old English inn says, "Fear knocked at the door. Faith answered; no one was there."

The older we grow, the more we come to grips with this thing called fear—fear of failing health, fear of the future, fear of the unknown, perhaps even fear of age itself.

The first thing we should remember is that fear is nothing to be ashamed of. On the other hand, uncontrolled fear is a poison that can paralyze and immobilize.

One antidote to fear is courage. Courage is not the absence of fear. It is the ability to go ahead in spite of fear. What is the source of courage like this? Its source is faith in God—faith in that power which created the universe and endowed it with such virtues as kindness and love.

Another antidote to fear is a healthy confidence in ourselves, a confidence which says, "With God's help, I can overcome my difficulties or find the patience and strength to endure them."

When fear knocks, let faith answer. With God's help we can overcome our fears.

## 97. JESUS' PRESCRIPTION FOR WORRY

So don't worry at all about having enough food and clothing. . . . your heavenly Father already knows perfectly well that you need them, and he will give them to you if you give him first place in your life and live as he wants you to (Matt. 6:31-33, *The Living Bible*).

## 98. THE MASTER'S WAY

*Not ours to know the reason*
  *Why unanswered is our prayer;*
*But ours to wait for God's own time*
  *To lift the cross we bear.*

*Not ours to know the reason*
  *Why from loved ones we must part,*
*But ours to live in faith and hope,*
  *Though bleeding to the heart.*

*Not ours to know the reason*
  *Why this anguish, strife, and pain,*

*But ours to know a crown of thorns*
*Sweet graces for us gain.*

*A cross, a bleeding heart, and crown—*
*What greater gifts are given?*
*Be still, my heart, and murmur not:*
*These are the keys to heaven.*

## 99. A DAY WELL SPENT

*If we sit down at set of sun*
*And count the things that we have done,*
*And counting, find*
*One self-denying act, one word*
*That eased the heart of one who heard;*
*One glance most kind*
*That fell like sunshine where it went—*
*Then we may count the day well spent.*

## 100. TIME

Suppose your bank credited your account each morning with $86,400, carried over no balance from day to day, and allowed you to keep no cash in your account. Then suppose that every evening the bank canceled out whatever you failed to use during the day.

All of us have such a bank. Its name is time. Every morning it credits us with 86,400 seconds. Every night it rules off as lost whatever time we have failed to invest for good during the day. It carries over no balance. It allows no overdrafts. Each day it opens up a new account. Each night it burns the records of the day. If you fail to use the day's deposits, the loss is yours.

There is no going back with time. There is no drawing against tomorrow. You must live in the present on today's deposits. Invest it in order to get from it the very best in health, happiness, and success.

## 101. THE WAY OF THE LORD

The following words were scribbled more than a century ago by a Confederate soldier:

I asked God for strength that I might achieve. I was made weak that I might learn humbly to obey.

I asked God for health that I might do greater things. I was given infirmity that I might do better things.

I asked for riches that I might be happy. I was given poverty that I might be wise.

I asked for all things that I might enjoy life. I was given life that I might enjoy all things.

I got nothing that I asked for but everything that I hoped for. Despite myself, my prayers were answered. I am, among men, most richly blessed!

## 102. GOD'S TEN MOST WANTED MEN

1. The man who puts God's business above any other business.
2. The man who brings his children to church rather than sends them.
3. The man who is willing to be the right example to every person whom he meets.
4. The man who thinks more of Sunday school than of Sunday sleep.
5. The man who gives what he should to the church and lives on what is left.
6. The man who goes to church for Christ's sake rather than for himself or someone else.
7. The man who has a passion to help others rather than to be helped himself.
8. The man who has a willing mind rather than a brilliant one.
9. The man who can see his own faults before he sees the faults of others.

10. The man who is more concerned about winning persons to Christ than about winning worldly honors.

## 103. THE MEANING OF WORSHIP

To worship is:
To quicken the conscience by the holiness of God.
To feed the mind with the truth of God.
To purge the imagination with the beauty of God.
To open the heart to the love of God.
To devote the will to the purpose of God.

—*William Temple*

## 104. OVERHEARD IN AN ORCHARD

*Said the robin to the sparrow,*
*"I should really like to know*
*Why these anxious human beings*
*Rush about and worry so?"*

*Said the sparrow to the robin,*
*"Friend, I think that it must be*
*That they have no heavenly Father*
*Such as cares for you and me."*

—Elizabeth Cheney

## 105. A SEVENTY-YEAR LIFE

Suppose God granted you a life of seventy years. How would you spend it? An average person would spend it like this:
   Three years getting an education.
   Eight years recreating and relaxing.
   Six years eating.
   Five years riding in a car.
   Four years talking.
   Fourteen years working.

Three years reading.
Twenty-four years sleeping.

How much time do you give to God? If you went to church every week and prayed for five minutes every morning and evening, you would give five months to God—five months out of seventy years.

## 106. TRUE WORSHIP

True worship is essential for effective evangelism.

True worship is essential for Christian maturity.

True worship will produce a concern for unsaved people.

True worship drives one to lead others to Christ.

True worship is more than sitting down and being passive and quiet. Worship is to be expressed through reaching out to others.

True worship leads all church members to witness daily.

## 107. LIFE

*God gives us each but one short day—*
*The time that we call life—*
*To waste or cherish as we will,*
*To spend in peace or strife.*

*One little day in which to do,*
*Or else to leave undone*
*The work He gives us. We must leave*
*It all at set of sun.*

*But one brief day in which to learn*
*That we are not our own;*
*That a day's sweetest pleasure*
*Is to hush another's moan.*

That life of selfish living
  Brings no blessed eventide,
While life of loving service
  Finds deep joy on every side.

But one brief day; oh, help me, Lord,
  To use it as I should!
Help me, for others, in that day
  To do some little good.

And when at twilight cool and dim
  I hear Thy gentle call,
Dear Lord, forgive me, if for thee
  I have not given You all.

# 6
# Stewardship and Church Finance

## 108. THE TITHER'S SURPRISES

The Christian who begins to tithe will be surprised:
1. At the amount of money he has for the Lord's work.
2. At the extent to which his own spiritual life deepens.
3. At the ease with which the nine-tenths that remains meets his own financial obligations.
4. At the ease with which he can give even more than one-tenth.
5. At the way in which tithing prepares him to be a faithful and wise steward over all his possessions.
6. At himself for not beginning to tithe sooner.

## 109. I AM GLAD MY CHURCH NEEDS MONEY

Have you ever heard anyone say: "My church is always asking for money. I wish I could belong to a church that never needed any money."

Surely they don't mean that. Any church that is alive needs money. Only dead churches do not call on their members for support. If anyone should accuse your church of always needing and calling for money, regard it as a compliment. Invite this person to rejoice with you that you both belong to a live, going concern of Jesus Christ rather than a dead, stagnant organization from which the glory of Christ has departed.

One father was complaining to another that his son cost him a great deal of money—for books, clothes, lunch, allowance, and tuition.

"It's strange that you feel that," the other father replied. "My son doesn't cost me a cent. I haven't spent a dime on him in over two years, but I sure wish I could."

"Why doesn't he cost you anything?" asked the first father.

The second father replied, "A little over two years ago he died."

A church that is alive needs the liberal, sacrificial support of those who love it. Only a dead church demands no sacrifice.

## 110. THE APOSTLE PAUL'S PLAN FOR CHURCH FINANCE

This plan for church finance is based on I Corinthians 16:2:

**Periodic:** Upon the first day of the week.

**Personal:** Let each one of you.

**Provident:** Lay by him in store.

**Proportionate:** As he may prosper.

**Preventive:** That no collections be made when I come.

## 111. LABORERS TOGETHER WITH GOD

One of the greatest truths of the Bible is that all Christians are "laborers together with God." This simply means that all members of our church are partners with God in His plan to give the gospel to the world.

All of us cannot go into all the world and preach the gospel to every creature. All of us cannot heal the sick, feed the orphans, and care for the aged. But we can have a part in all these activities by giving our tithes and offerings to the church every week. As we give, the grace of God flows through the lives of thousands of other people everywhere.

Christian stewardship is all of us working in partnership with God to proclaim His "good news" throughout the world.

## 112. THE LESSONS OF TITHING

Tithing teaches at least eight great spiritual lessons:
1. Dependence upon God in every phase of life.
2. Reverence for all that belongs to God.
3. The joy of helping in a worldwide mission program.
4. Concern for lost people everywhere.
5. Systematic handling of God's work.
6. Faith in God and His promises.
7. Liberality of heart and hand.
8. The proper place of money in one's life.

## 113. THE STEWARD'S PRAYER

*Ah, when I look up at the cross*
*Where God's Steward suffered loss*
*Of life, and shed His blood for me;*
*Oh, trifling thing it seems to be*
*To pay a tithe, dear Lord, to Thee,*
*Of time, or talent, wealth, or store,*
*Full well I know I owe Thee more;*
*A million times I owe Thee more!*

*But that is just the reason why*
*I lift my heart to God on high*
*And pledge Thee, by this portion small,*
*My life, my love, my all in all.*
*This holy token at Thy cross*

*I know as gold, must seem but dross,*
*But in my heart, Lord, Thou dost see*
*How it was pledged in love to Three;*
*That I a steward true may be.*
                                    —R. S. Cushman

## 114. THE SEVENFOLD BLESSING OF THE TITHE

1. It blesses the **heart** by making it receptive to God's will.
2. It blesses the **life** by lifting it to a higher plane of grace.
3. It blesses the **hands** by making them willing to do God's work.
4. It blesses the **mind** by giving it the satisfaction of doing the right thing.
5. It blesses the **nine-tenths** that remains because God has been honored.
6. It blesses the **individual** by giving him a part in God's worldwide program of work.
7. It blesses the **church** by enabling it to carry out a greater ministry.

## 115. DEFINITION OF A CHURCH BUDGET

The budget of our church is more than a set of figures or a list or expenditures. It is actually the program of the church.

It is the pastor preaching, visiting the sick, comforting the bereaved, winning the lost.

It is the Sunday school teaching the Word of God to the multitudes.

It is the organ playing and the choir singing to the glory of God.

It is the church building, standing as a lighthouse in the midst of a dark world.

It is missionaries sent to foreign lands to preach the good news of Jesus Christ.

It is Christian literature in the hands of a child.

It is schools, hospitals, and children's homes, ministering to those in need.

Most of all, perhaps, the budget of our church is the total expression of our love for Christ, our compassion for a lost world, and our realization that God will hold each of us accountable for our stewardship.

## 116. THE MESSAGE OF MY MONEY

My money is really another pair of feet to walk today where Christ would walk if He were still on earth.

My money is another pair of hands to heal and feed and bless the desperate families of the earth.

My money is a prayer of intercession suddenly crossing time and space to help answer itself in one swift, unselfish gesture.

My money is one big part of my Christian life. If my money is not committed to Christ, then I am not totally dedicated to Jesus and His will.

## 117. HOW TO SUPPORT A CHURCH

The treasurer of a church resigned. Another man, the manager of a local grain elevator, was asked to take the position. He agreed to do so if, for one full year, the church would require no report from him and no one would ask him any questions about the church's finances.

The church members were puzzled at this strange request, but they finally granted it. Most of them had him process their grain, so they knew he was an honest man.

At the end of the year the new treasurer gave a glowing report. The church's indebtedness of $25,000 on the building had been paid in full. The pastor's salary had been increased. There were no outstanding bills, and there was even a cash balance of $12,000.

The pleasantly surprised congregation wanted an explanation.

"Most of you bring your grain to my elevator," the man replied. "When I paid you, I simply withheld ten percent on your behalf and gave it to the church in your name. You never missed it. Do you see what we could do for the Lord if we were willing to give the first tithe to God, who really owns it?"

## 118. THREE KICKS IN EVERY DOLLAR

William Allen White, a famous newspaper editor in Emporia, Kansas, used to say that there are "three kicks in every dollar." A great many people have discovered the first two kicks, but far too few know about the third.

In delivering the deed to a fifty-acre wooded tract for a city park, White once said: "This is the last kick in a fistful of dollars I am getting rid of. I have tried to teach people there are three kicks in every dollar: One when you make it—and how I do love to make a dollar! One when you save it—and I have the Yankee lust for saving. The third kick is when you give it away—and the biggest kick of all is that last one."

# 7
# New Year's Messages

## 119. I AM THE NEW YEAR

I am the new year. I am an unspoiled page in your book of time.

I am your next chance at the art of living.

I am your opportunity to practice what you have learned about life during the last twelve months.

All that you sought and didn't find is hidden in me, waiting for you to search it out with more determination.

All the good that you tried for and didn't achieve is mine to grant when you have fewer conflicting desires.

All that you dreamed but didn't dare to do, all that you hoped but did not will, all the faith that you claimed but did not have—these slumber lightly, waiting to be awakened by the touch of a strong purpose.

I am your opportunity to renew your allegiance to Him who said, "Behold, I make all things new." I am the new year.

## 120. SOME SUGGESTED RESOLUTIONS FOR THE NEW YEAR

During the new year I will:

Work hard. I will do the hardest job first every day.

Study hard. The more I know, the more effective my work becomes.

Have initiative. Ruts often deepen into graves.

Like what I do. There's a sense of satisfaction in doing work well.

Be exact. Accuracy is better than haste.

Have courage. A stout heart will carry me through many difficulties.

Be friendly. Only friendly people become successful leaders.

Cultivate personality. Personality is to persons what perfume is to flowers.

Wear a smile. A smile opens the door into the sunshine beyond.

Do my best. If you give to the world the best you have, the best will come back to you.


## 121. SOME NEW YEAR'S RESOLUTIONS WORTH KEEPING

During the new year:

I resolve to put Christ before my church and my church before my club.

I resolve to put the spiritual before the material and the eternal before the temporal.

I resolve to put God's Word before men's opinions.

I resolve to put Christ before the creed.

I resolve to put prayer before pleasure.

I resolve to put the Savior before the teacher. I resolve to walk more by faith and trust and less by sight and reason.

I resolve to live in order to give rather than to get.

I resolve to strive to be good rather than great.

I resolve to put more of God and less of myself in my work.

## 122. A DEFINITION OF THE NEW YEAR

*The new year is a door*
*By which we reach new fields*
*Of service for God and fellow man:*
*A door by which we can explore*
*Wide spheres of usefulness*
*Our world to bless,*
*And reap the sheaves God's word of witness yields.*

*The new year is a task*
*Set by the Master of our souls,*
*A little part of our life's work below:*
*And so we ask holy wisdom which alone controls*
*Our labor, teaching what and where to sow:*
*That the year, at its end,*
*May show God's glory and man's profit blend.*

*The new year is a book*
*With many pages, and as yet all white*
*On which to write*
*The history of thought, and deed, and word*
*In this new group of days.*
*We pray thee, Lord,*
*As thou shalt look upon the book,*
*When written over, may all be to Thy praise.*

## 123. THE GATE OF THE NEW YEAR

*And I said to the man*
*Who stood at the gate of the year:*

79

*"Give me a light,*
*That I may tread safely into the unknown."*

*And he replied:*
*"Go out into the darkness,*
*And put your hand into the hand of God.*
*That shall be to you better than light*
*And safer than the known way."*

*So I went forth and, finding the hand of God,*
*Trod gladly into the night.*
*And He led me toward the hills*
*And the breaking of the day in the lone East.*

*So heart, be still:*
*What need our little life,*
*Our human life, to know,*
*If God hath comprehension.*
*In all the dizzy strife*
*Of things both high and low,*
*God hideth His intention.*

—M. Louise Haskins

## 124. FAMOUS CHURCH PEOPLE OF THE YEAR

Various groups and organizations select their "Man of the Year." Perhaps it would be interesting if churches did the same.

**Church Member of the Year**—the one who has not missed a Wednesday night prayer service.

**Sunday School Director of the Year**—the one who gives his teachers plenty of time to teach God's Word instead of using it up during the devotional period.

**Teacher of the Year**—the one who sees his responsibility extending beyond the Sunday school class period.

**Soloist of the Year**—the one who is more concerned about the message of the song than the projection and pitch of his voice.

**Usher of the Year**—the one who seats people where they want to sit and keeps the temperature in the auditorium just where everybody wants it.

**Custodian of the Year**—the one who makes every spot of dirt disappear by Sunday morning at 9:30 A.M.

**Church Secretary of the Year**—the one who is always caught up with her work.

**Pastor of the Year**—the one who pleases all the people all the time.

## 125. SIX RESOLUTIONS FOR THE NEW YEAR

During the new year I resolve to:

Forget the past and honor God more.

Live for Christ in the world.

Trust God with a strong faith.

Remain faithful to my church.

Witness to the lost.

Cultivate whatever talents God has given me for His glory and His church.

## 126. THOUGHTS FOR THE NEW YEAR

*The new year lies before you*
*Like a spotless tract of snow;*
*Be careful how you tread on it*
*For every mark will show.*

## 127. RECIPE FOR A HAPPY NEW YEAR

Take twelve whole months. Clean them thoroughly of all bitterness, hate, and jealousy. Make them just as fresh and clean as possible.

Now cut each month into twenty-eight, thirty, or thirty-one different parts, but don't make up the whole batch at once. Prepare it one day at a time out of these ingredients.

Mix well into each day one part of faith, one part of patience, one part of courage, and one part of work. Add to each day one part of hope, faithfulness, generosity, and kindness. Blend with one part prayer, one part meditation, and one good deed. Season the whole with a dash of good spirits, a sprinkle of fun, a pinch of play, and a cupful of good humor.

Pour all of this into a vessel of love. Cook thoroughly over radiant joy, garnish with a smile, and serve with quietness, unselfishness, and cheerfulness. You're bound to have a happy new year.

## 128. TEN NEW YEAR'S QUESTIONS
## FOR THE CHRISTIAN

Take a look at yourself as the new year begins. Consider these questions:

1. What has been your record in your church during the past year?
2. What were your happiest Christian experiences?
3. Do you feel that Christian achievement is worth the effort?
4. Have you paid in service for the guidance you have recieved from others?
5. Do you feel that every person has a share in the Lord's work?
6. Will you place the Lord's favor above personal satisfaction?
7. Will you seek God's will for your life in your daily prayer and meditation?
8. Will you accept a church job that requires your talent, that requires you best?
9. Will you pray daily that the Lord will burden you and your fellow Christians concerning your Christian responsibilities?
10. Will you pray definitely for these needs?

## 129. SOME NEW YEAR'S WISHES FOR YOU

During the new year may you have:

Enough happiness to keep you sweet.

Enough trials to keep you strong.

Enough sorrow to keep you human.

Enough hope to keep you happy.

Enough failure to keep you humble.

Enough success to keep you eager.

Enough friends to give you comfort.

Enough wealth to meet your needs.

Enough enthusiasm to make you look forward to tomorrow.

Enough determination to make each day better than the day before.

## 130. A BRIDGE FOR OTHERS

*An old man, traveling a lone highway,*
*Came at the evening, cold and gray,*
*To a chasm vast and deep and wide.*
*The old man crossed in the twilight dim—*
*The sullen stream had no fear for him;*
*But he turned, when safe on the other side*
*And built a bridge to span the tide.*

*"Old man," said a pilgrim standing near,*
*"You are wasting your strength in building here;*
*Your journey will end with the closing day;*
*You never again will pass this way.*
*You have crossed the chasm deep and wide;*
*Why build this bridge at eventide?"*

*The builder lifted his old gray head:*
*"Good friend, in the path I've come," he said,*
*"There followeth after me today*

*A youth whose feet must pass this way;*
*The chasm that has been as naught to me*
*To that fair-haired youth may a pitfall be;*
*He too must cross in the twilight dim—*
*Good friend, I'm building this bridge for him."*

## 131. SOME CHRISTIAN RESOLUTIONS FOR THE NEW YEAR

During the new year I will:

Like **Paul,** forget those things which are behind and press forward.

Like **David,** lift up my eyes to the hills from which my help comes.

Like **Abraham,** trust my God implicitly.

Like **Enoch,** walk in daily fellowship with my heavenly Father.

Like **Moses,** suffer rather than enjoy the pleasure of sin for a time.

Like **Job,** be patient and faithful in all circumstances.

Like **Joseph,** turn my back on all evil advances.

Like **Gideon,** advance even when my friends are few.

Like **Andrew,** strive to lead my brother to Christ.

## 132. A PRAYER FOR THE NEW YEAR

*Lord, make me an instrument of Thy peace;*
*Where there is hatred, let me sow love;*
*Where there is injury, pardon;*
*Where there is doubt, faith;*
*Where there is despair, hope;*
*Where there is darkness, light;*
*Where there is sadness, joy.*

*O divine master, grant that I may not so much*
*Seek to be consoled as to console;*
*To be understood as to understand;*
*To be loved as to love.*

*For it is in giving that we receive;*
*It is in pardoning that we are pardoned;*
*It is in dying that we are born to eternal life.*
                                        —St. Francis of Assisi

# 8
# Thanksgiving Messages

---

### 133. A THANKSGIVING PRAYER

*Father, we thank Thee for the night*
*And for the pleasant morning light,*
*For rest and food and loving care*
*And all that makes the day so fair.*

*Help us to do the things we should;*
*To be to others kind and good;*
*In all we do in work or play,*
*To grow more loving every day.*

### 134. A PSALM OF THANKSGIVING

Make a joyful noise unto the Lord, all ye lands.

Serve the Lord with gladness: come before His presence with singing.

Know ye that the Lord He is God: it is He that hath made us, and not we ourselves; we are His people, and the sheep of His pasture.

Enter into His gates with thanksgiving, and into His courts with praise: be thankful unto Him, and bless His name.

For the Lord is good; His mercy is everlasting; and His truth endureth to all generations.                              (Ps. 100)


## 135. MEDITATIONS FOR THANKSGIVING

Even though I clutch my blanket and growl when the alarm rings every morning, thank you, Lord, that I can hear; there are many who are deaf.

Even though I keep my eyes tightly closed against the morning light as long as possible, thank you, Lord, that I can see; there are many who are blind.

Even though I huddle in my bed and put off getting up, thank you, Lord, that I have strength to rise; there are many who are bedfast.

Even though the first hour of my day is hectic—socks are lost, toast is burned, and tempers are short—thank you, Lord, for my family; there are many who are lonely.

Even though our breakfast table never looks like those in the ladies' magazines and the menu is sometimes unbalanced, thank you, Lord, for the food we have; there are those who are hungry.

Even though my job is often monotonous, thank you, Lord, for the opportunity to work; there are many who are out of work.

Even though I grumble from day to day and wish my circumstances were not quite so modest, thank you, Lord, for the gift of life!


## 136. LET OUR LIVES BE OUR THANKSGIVING

*Let our lives be our Thanksgiving*
*To our Father up above;*

*Let us worship Him with kindness;*
*Let us praise Him with our love.*

*Let us honor Him with virtue;*
*Let good deeds become our prayer;*
*Let our lives be our Thanksgiving*
*For the bounty that we share.*

## 137. SOME THINGS TO REMEMBER AT THANKSGIVING

A great deal has been written about the virtue of forgetting old grudges, prejudices, unpleasant experiences, and heartaches. We also need to be reminded of some of the blessings of remembering. Remembering can be good spiritual exercise. At Thanksgiving we need to:

Remember **our sins** that we might confess them to God.

Remember **our weaknesses** that we may receive strength.

Remember **our humanity** that we might stop trying to be God.

Remember **God's mercies** that we might be merciful to others.

Remember **our joys** that we might be joyful.

Remember **God's greatness** that we might be humble.

Remember **our poverty** that we might share our prosperity.

Remember **God's forgiveness** that we might forgive others.

Remember **our needs** that we might serve the needs of others.

Remember **Jesus Christ** that we might grow to be more like Him.

## 138. HOW TO OBSERVE THANKSGIVING

*Count your blessings instead of your crosses;*
*Count your gains instead of your losses.*
*Count your joys instead of your woes;*

*Count your friends instead of your foes.*
*Count your smiles instead of your tears;*
*Count your courage instead of your fears.*
*Count your full years instead of your lean;*
*Count your kind deeds instead of your mean.*
*Count your health instead of your wealth;*
*Count on God instead of yourself.*

# 9
# Christmas
# Messages

---

## 139. DAILY BIBLE READINGS
## FOR THE CHRISTMAS SEASON

December 24: The message of cheer. Isaiah 40: 1-11.
December 25: The message of peace. Hosea 14:1-9.
December 26: The message of redemption. Revelation 5:1-14.
December 27: The Word and the world. John 1:1-14.
December 28: The first Christmas service. Luke 2:8-17.
December 29: Good tidings. Psalm 86:1-10.
December 30: The sustaining gift. John 6:22-35.
December 31: The immeasurable gift. John 3:23-36.

## 140. YOU CAN KEEP CHRISTMAS

Are you willing to believe that love is the strongest thing in the world—stronger than hate, stronger than evil, stronger than death—and that the blessed life which began in Bethlehem two thousand years ago is the image and brightness of the eternal love? Then you can keep Christmas.

## 141. A CHRISTMAS WISH

*May*
*the warm,*
*guiding star*
*drive from your*
*life every shadow;*
*may the glad song of*
*angels find an echo in*
*your heart; may the spirit*
*of worship in the hearts of*
*the wise men, and the simple*
*faith of the shepherds be yours*
*as, once more, you celebrate the*
*birth-*
*day of*
*the King*

## 142. A CHILD'S CHRISTMAS LETTER TO JESUS

In 1972 an eight-year-old girl at Bellevue Baptist Church, Memphis, Tennessee, wrote the following Christmas letter to Jesus:

> Dear Jesus:
>
> My name is Cathy. I am eight. Mommy said I should write a letter to Santa Claus, but I decided to write you first, 'cause I know Christmas is your birthday. I just wanted to write happy birthday. I hope you get lots of presents like I got at my party.
>
> I asked my Mommy where to send a letter to Jesus. She wouldn't answer me. But I think if I just wrote Jesus on the outside of the envelope the postman will know where to take it.
>
> Daddy gave me $3.00 to buy presents with. I'll buy you the biggest, 'cause it's your birthday. I don't even know what you want. Please drop me a little hint.
>
> Your friend,
> Cathy

Mrs. Thurman Prewett, director of the Sunday school department in which Cathy was enrolled, wrote the following response to Cathy's letter:

Dear Cathy:

Your letter to Jesus is one of the finest letters I have ever read. I agree with you, Cathy. Buying a gift for Jesus is very hard to do. In fact, even if you had all the dollars in the world, I doubt if you could buy a present fine enough for Jesus. But there is one thing that Jesus wants very much. He wants you, Cathy. He loves you, and He wants you to love Him. Your best gift, Cathy, is you. I think that kind of present would give Jesus a most happy birthday!

## 143. I LIKE CHRISTMAS

I like Christmas! Christmas is something new that comes each year to an old world. It is like new-fallen snow upon an old tree; a new flower on an old plant; new shoes on aging feet; a new home in an old town; a new light on a dark street; new hope in a hopeless situation.

I like Christmas! It was introduced by a prophecy, heralded by the song of an angel, and announced by the birth of the Savior.

I like Christmas because it sparkles and glows. It comes only once a year, and still its radiance warms the child's heart and fills his mind with pleasant dreams of joy and happiness.

I like Christmas because Christmas is Christ. In Christ I see the beauty of the gospel which began in Bethlehem of Judea when His spirit glorified that little town and His coming sanctified a lowly manger.

I like Christmas because it bears Christ's name, symbolizes His love, proclaims His truth, and showers His gifts upon the world. Although earthly kings ignored Him and the proud could not understand Him, the common people heard Him with hungry hearts and gladly received Him.

I like Christmas because it meets my deepest needs! It cures me of greed and selfishness, fills my empty soul with peace and compassion, and renews my faith and hope in an erring world.

These are some of the reasons why I like Christmas!

## 144. THE REAL MEANING OF CHRISTMAS

*May Christmas time mean more to you*
*Than gifts on Christmas morn;*
*May you feel the peace the whole world knew*
*When Christ the Lord was born!*

*May you know the special gladness*
*And hope that came to men;*
*And may it thrill your heart just now*
*As Christmas comes again!*

## 145. SOME DEFINITIONS OF CHRISTMAS

Christmas is the **light** that burns eternally. It is a glow that warms the hearts of people wherever the message of "Peace on earth to men of goodwill" is believed.

Christmas is **peace** in a world where people have been alienated from each other by hatred and jealousy.

Christmas is **love** that flows from one heart to another.

Christmas is the **joy** of brotherhood, of giving, of sharing, of lifting, of caring, and of being what Christ wants us to be.

Christmas is **forgiveness,** the time for fresh beginnings, a time to right the wrongs of yesterday.

Christmas is **giving** to those who cannot give to us. It is visiting the neglected, lifting the fallen, giving hope to the hopeless, assuring victory to the defeated, living the spirit of good will to all mankind.

Christmas is **surrender** of one's life to Christ in renewed dedication, making Christ the Lord of our lives.

## 146. ONE SOLITARY LIFE

He was born in an obscure village, the child of a peasant woman. He grew up in still another village, where He worked in a carpenter shop until He was thirty. Then for three years He was an itinerant preacher. He never wrote a book. He never held an office. He never had a family or owned a house. He didn't go to college. He never visited a big city.

He never traveled more than two hundred miles from the place where He was born. He did none of the things one usually associates with greatness. He had no credentials but Himself. He was only thirty-three when the tide of public opinion turned against him. His friends ran away.

He was turned over to His enemies and went through the mockery of a trial. He was nailed to a cross between two thieves. While He was dying, His executioners gambled for His clothing, the only property He had on earth. After He died, He was laid in a borrowed grave through the pity of a friend.

Nineteen centuries have come and gone, and today He is the central figure of the human race and the leader of mankind's progress. All the armies that ever marched, all the navies that ever sailed, all the parliaments that ever sat, all the kings that ever reigned, put together, have not affected the life of man on this earth as much as that one solitary life.

## 147. CHRISTMAS WORDS

*joy*
*grace*
*hope—love*
*faith—peace*
*honor—purity*
*justice—charity*
*courage—loyalty*
*goodness—prudence*
*sympathy—humility*
*fortitude—temperance*
*brotherhood—cooperation*
*and*
*God*
*is*
*love*

## 148. HOW TO KEEP CHRISTMAS

Are you willing:

> To stoop down and consider the needs and desires of little children?

> To remember the weakness and loneliness of people who are growing old?

> To stop asking how much your friends love you and to ask yourself whether you love them enough?

> To bear in mind the things that other people have to bear on their hearts?

> To trim your lamp so that it will give more light and less smoke, and to carry it in front so that your shadow will fall behind you?

> To make a grave for your ugly thoughts and a garden for your kindly feelings?

Are you willing to do these things for a day? If you are, then you are ready to keep Christmas!

*—Henry Van Dyke*


## 149. SAME OLD CHRISTMAS STUFF

The department store Santas are at it again, saying "Ho, ho, ho" to the children and patting them gently on their little heads.

Go shopping in some people-to-people-covered store, and get stuck with some inexperienced clerk who never heard of sizes and doesn't know how to wrap a package.

Then come home to the same old tree. Turn on the radio or television and hear the same old carols. Hide the gifts in the same old places. Send Christmas cards to the same old people.

Honestly, it's the same old stuff all over again—the same kind of hints from the family, the same childish stockings hung up, the same kind of candy, the same mistletoe jokes, the same colored lights strung on the porch, the same wreath in the window, the same fuss and bother visiting relatives and friends.

Yes, it's the same old stuff.

At last the waiting is over; the gifts are opened; the oh's and ah's are expressed; the wrappings are gathered up and put in the garbage. Then the misty-eyed thank-you's start, and everyone begins reminiscing about past Christmas get-togethers.

When the sentimental nonsense stops and there are a few seconds of silence, somebody is sure to pop up again with "Merry Christmas" or "Peace on earth, good will toward men."

Same old stuff.

Same old wonderful, marvelous stuff!

## 150. CHRISTMAS IS . . .

*joy,*
*bells,*
*winter,*
*mistletoe,*
*visits, smiles,*
*manger, love,*
*laughter, wreath,*
*baby, star, caroler,*
*snow, peace, Santa Claus,*
*sharing, pine cones, candles,*
*Tiny Tim, "Old Scrooge," children,*
*and Jesus,*
*God's Son,*
*who died*
*for our sins*

## 151. GOD'S CHRISTMAS GIFT

The tag—"For unto you is born this day in the city of David a Saviour, which is Christ the Lord" (Luke 2:11).

**The wrapping**—"And this shall be a sign unto you; ye shall find the babe wrapped in swaddling clothes, lying in a manger" (Luke 2:12).

**The trimmings**—"And suddenly there was with the angel a multitude of the heavenly host praising God, and saying, Glory to God in the highest, and on earth peace, good will toward men" (Luke 2:13, 14).

**The contents**—"But when the fulness of the time was come, God sent forth his Son, made of a woman, made under the law, to redeem them that were under the law, that we might receive the adoption of sons" (Gal. 4:4, 5).

**Gratitude**—"Thanks be unto God for his unspeakable gift" (II Cor. 9:15).

## 152. HIS NAME AT THE TOP

*I had the nicest Christmas list—*
*The longest one in town—*
*Til Daddy looked at it and said,*
*"You'll have to cut it down."*

*I knew that what he said was true*
*Beyond the faintest doubt,*
*But I was amazed to hear him say,*
*"You've left your best friend out."*

*And so I scanned my list again,*
*And said, "Oh, that's not true!"*
*But Daddy said, "His name's not there—*
*That Friend who died for you."*

*And then I clearly understood*
*'Twas Jesus that he meant;*
*For Him who should come first of all*
*I hadn't planned a cent.*

*I had made a lengthy Christmas list*
*And left the Savior out!*
*But, oh, it didn't take me long*
*To change the list about.*

*And though I've had to drop some names*
  *Of folks I like a lot;*
*My Lord must have the most—because—*
  *His name is at the top.*

## 153. SOME CHRISTMAS REMINDERS

May the Christmas **gifts** remind you of God's greatest gift, His only begotten Son.

May the Christmas **candles** remind you of Him who is the "Light of the world."

May the Christmas **trees** remind you of another tree upon which He died for you.

May the Christmas **cheer** remind you of Him who said, "Be of good cheer."

May the Christmas **bell** remind you of the glorious proclamation of His birth.

May the Christmas **carols** remind you of the song the angels sang, "Glory to God in the highest."

May the Christmas **season** remind you in every way of Jesus Christ your King.

## 154. IF I WERE GOD . . .

If I were God; oh, if only I were God—I would be in every hospital room where a person is being told that he has a terminal illness, and I would give him courage. Then I would sponsor a healing and invite all the sick of the earth. I would comfort every family where death has occurred. And, by some miracle, I would plan a resurrection.

If I were God; oh, if only I were God—I would have a banquet and invite all the hungry children in this world. Then I would help every child's father find a job. I would attend the board meeting of the power makers and veto the actions that manipulate the oppressed.

If I were God; oh, if only I were God—I would build a big bonfire to attract all the cold people. Then I would give them warm clothes for the winter, clean clothes for school and work, and bright clothes for parties. I would do something about the intolerable physical conditions under which they live.

If I were God; oh, if only I were God—I would put on a celebration of dignity and ask all who feel badly about themselves to come, whether rich or poor. I would send engraved invitations to the prisoners and tell them how much worth they have in my sight. Then I would put them with others who have the same insight.

If I were God; oh, if only I were God—I would start a "peace" everywhere there is a war, and where wars of liberation are necessary I would turn back time itself and correct the conditions that led to such desperate action. Where war had already strewn its carnage, I would stand beside every homeless child and comfort every mother who had lost her children.

All these things I would do if only I were God. But send my son into an obscure part of this world and tell him to show a few people what redemptive love is—knowing that he would be killed—and trust them to take up my work?

Never!                                              —*G. Temp Sparkman*

# 10
# The Bible and Its Message

---

## 155. DIARY OF A BIBLE

**January**: A busy time for me. Most of the family decided to read me through this year. They kept me busy for the first two weeks, but they have forgotten me now.

**February**: Clean-up time. I was dusted yesterday and put in my place. My owner did use me for a few minutes last week. He had been in an argument and was looking up some references to prove he was right.

**March**: I had a busy day the first of the month. My owner was elected president of the P.T.A., and he used me to prepare a speech.

**April**: Grandpa visited us this month. He kept me on his lap for an hour reading I Corinthians 13. He seems to think more of me than do some people in my own household.

**May**: I have a few green stains on my pages. Some spring flowers were pressed in my pages.

**June:** I look like a scrapbook. They have stuffed me full of newspaper clippings—one of the girls was married.

**July:** They put me in a suitcase today. I guess we are off on vacation. I wish I could stay home; I know I'll be closed up in this thing for at least two weeks.

**August:** Still in the suitcase.

**September:** Back home at last and in my old familiar place. I have a lot of company. Two women's magazines and four comic books are stacked on top of me. I wish I could be read as much as they are.

**October:** They read me a little bit today. One of them is very sick. Right now I am sitting in the center of the coffee table. I think the pastor is coming by for a visit.

**November:** Back in my old place. Somebody asked today if I were a scrapbook.

**December:** The family is busy getting ready for the holidays. I guess I'll be covered up under wrapping paper and packages again—just as I am every Christmas.


## 156. THE BIBLE: THE BOOK OF BOOKS

The Bible reveals the mind of God, the state of man, the way of life, the doom of sinners, and the happiness of believers. Read it to be wise. Believe it to be safe. Practice it to be holy.

It gives light to direct you, food to support you, and comfort to cheer you. It is the traveler's map, the soldier's sword, the Christian's chart.

In the Bible paradise is restored; heaven is opened; and the gates of hell are described. Christ is its theme, our good its design, and the glory of God its purpose.

The Bible should fill our memories, rule our hearts, and guide our feet. Read it slowly, frequently, and prayerfully.

It is a mine of wealth, a paradise of glory, a river of pleasure. It is given to us in life; it will be open in judgment and remembered forever. It involves the highest responsibility, rewards the greatest labor, and condemns all who trifle with it.

The Bible sets forth two things—the cross and the throne. The Old Testament points toward the cross. The Gospels tell the story of the cross. The Epistles point toward the throne. The Book of Revelation tells the story of the throne.

The Old Testament tells us what sin leads to and ends with: "Lest I come and smite the earth with a curse" (Mal. 4:6).

The New Testament shows the way out of sin and ends like this: "The grace of our Lord Jesus Christ be with you all" (Rev. 22:21).

*—From the flyleaf of Dwight L. Moody's Bible*

## 157. THE GOSPEL IN MINIATURE: JOHN 3:16

God: The greatest lover.
So loved: The greatest degree.
The world: The greatest company.
That he gave: The greatest act.
His only begotten Son: The greatest gift.
That whosoever: The greatest opportunity.
Believeth: The greatest simplicity.
In Him: The greatest attraction.
Should not perish: The greatest promise.
But: The greatest difference.
Have: The greatest certainty.
Everlasting life: The greatest possession.

## 158. I AM THE BIBLE

I am the Bible, God's wonderful library. I am always—and above all—the truth.

To the weary pilgrim, I am a strong staff.

To the one who sits in darkness, I am glorious light.

To those who stumble beneath heavy burdens, I am sweet rest.

To him who has lost his way, I am a safe guide.

To those who are sick in sin, I am healing strength and forgiveness.

To the discouraged, I am a glad message of hope.

To those who are distressed and tossed about by the storms of life, I am an anchor, sure and steadfast.

To those who search for salvation, I reveal the Savior of the world.

I am the Bible.

## 159. SOME MESSAGES FROM THE BIBLE

When in sorrow, read John 14.
When men fail you, read Psalm 27.
When you have sinned, read Psalm 51.
When you worry, read Matthew 6:19-34.
When you are in danger, read Psalm 91.
When you have the blues, read Psalm 34.
When God seems far away, read Psalm 139.
If you are discouraged, read Isaiah 40.
If you are lonely or fearful, read Psalm 23.
If you feel down and out, read Romans 8:38, 39.
If you need courage, read Joshua 1.
If the world seems bigger than God, read Psalm 90.
If you want rest and peace, read Matthew 11:25-30.
If you get bitter or critical, read I Corinthians 13.
For a great invitation, read Isaiah 55.

## 160. ABUNDANT LIFE
## FROM AN ABUNDANT SHEPHERD

The world's favorite Psalm promises abundance. The infinite storehouse is God Himself. As the Psalmist expressed it, "The Lord is my shepherd, I shall not want." According to the Psalmist, the Good Shepherd provides:

**Food:** He maketh me to lie down in green pastures.

**Water:** He leadeth me beside the still waters.

**Refreshment:** He restoreth my soul.

**Guidance:** He leadeth me in the paths of righteousness.

**Assurance:** Yea, though I walk through the valley of the shadow of death.

**Freedom from fear:** I will fear no evil.

**Fellowship:** For thou art with me.

**Discipline:** Thy rod.

**Rescue:** And thy staff.

**Comfort:** They comfort me.

**Prosperity:** Thou preparest a table before me in the presence of mine enemies.

**Healing:** Thou anointest my head with oil.

**Joy:** My cup runneth over.

**Triumphant faith:** Surely goodness and mercy shall follow me.

**Confidence:** All the days of my life.

**Inheritance:** And I will dwell in the house of the Lord for ever.


## 161. LEARN FROM GREAT BIBLE PERSONALITIES

If you are impatient, sit down and talk with Job.

If you are just a little strong-headed, go and see Moses.

If you are tired and afraid, take a good look at Elijah.

If there is no song in your heart, listen to David.

If you feel cold and lonely, get the beloved disciple John to put his arm around you.

If your faith is weak, read about the apostle Paul.

If you are getting lazy, listen to James.

If you are losing sight of the future, climb up the stairs of Revelation and get a glimpse of the promised land.

## 162. COMFORT FOR THE WEARY

Come unto me, all ye that labour and are heavy laden, and I will give you rest. Take my yoke upon you, and learn of me; for I am meek and lowly in heart: and ye shall find rest unto your souls. For my yoke is easy, and my burden is light (Matt. 11:28-30).

## 163. THE PERFECT PSALM

**Perfect salvation:** The Lord is my shepherd.
**Perfect satisfaction:** I shall not want.
**Perfect rest:** He maketh me to lie down in green pastures.
**Perfect refreshment:** He leadeth me beside the still waters.
**Perfect restoration:** He restoreth my soul.
**Perfect guidance:** He leadeth me in the paths of righteousness.
**Perfect protection:** I will fear no evil.
**Perfect company:** Thou art with me.
**Perfect provision:** Thou preparest a table.
**Perfect consecration:** Thou anointest my head.
**Perfect joy:** My cup runneth over.
**Perfect care:** Goodness and mercy shall follow me.
**Perfect destiny:** I will dwell in the house of the Lord for ever.

## 164. THE BIBLE SPEAKS—

About sin:

"For all have sinned, and come short of the glory of God" (Rom. 3:23).

"And God saw that the wickedness of man was great in the

earth, and that every imagination of the thoughts of his heart was only evil continually" (Gen. 6:5).

About the way of salvation:

"Neither is there salvation in any other: for there is none other name under heaven given among men, whereby we must be saved" (Acts 4:12).

About repentance and confession:

"If we confess our sins, he is faithful and just to forgive us our sins, and to cleanse us from all unrighteousness" (I John 1:9).

"I acknowledged my sin unto thee, and mine iniquity have I not hid. I said, I will confess my transgressions unto the Lord; and thou forgavest the iniquity of my sin" (Ps. 32:5).

# 11
# Music, Choirs, and Congregational Singing

## 165. TEN COMMANDMENTS FOR CHOIR MEMBERS

1. Thou shalt have no other activities or committee meetings before thee at choir rehearsal time.
2. Thou shalt not make unto the choir director any weak excuses for missing rehearsal.
3. Thou shalt not use the rehearsal time to talk and joke with thy neighbors, for the rehearsal time is limited.
4. Remember the rehearsal time to keep thyself prompt.
5. Honor thy Lord and thy heavenly Father for the talent He gavest thee to be used for His glory.
6. Thou shalt not kill the harmony of the group by singing off key.
7. Thou shalt not ignore the director's instructions and requests.
8. Thou shalt not steal thy neighbor's notes when singing separate parts.
9. Thou shalt not bear false witness by acting as though thou knowest more about the music than the director.
10. Thou shalt not covet the talents of the other members

of the choir, nor the position of the choir director, nor the chief seat in the choir loft.

## 166. A MESSAGE FOR CHOIR MEMBERS

*You are the chosen of the Lord*
*To sing His highest praise;*
*And through the medium of song*
*To show His wondrous ways.*

*Yours is the privilege of grace;*
*Your words His truth express;*
*Through sacred music you promote*
*The cause of righteousness.*

*So lift your voice with one accord*
*And let your anthems ring;*
*The people will be richly blessed,*
*And God will hear you sing.*

## 167. THE KEY OF C

Members of the choirs who sing in our worship services should always sing in the perfect key of C:

**Converted** to new life in Jesus Christ.

**Concrete** in testimony.

**Confessing** Christ at every opportunity of service in song.

**Confident** of their hope in Christ.

**Crystal-like** in radiating His testimony.

**Consistent** in fulfilling their responsibility.

**Concentrating** on making Christ known through song.

**Concerned** about doing their best for His glory.

**Consecrated** to the Christian task which is theirs.

**Cooperative** in spirit.

## 168. DO WE REALLY MEAN WHAT WE SING?

The singing of a hymn should be a great experience for Christians. A hymn can be a prayer, a testimony, praise, or an invitation to others. Many of us apparently don't take the words we sing very seriously.

We sing "Sweet Hour of Prayer" and pray only a few minutes each day.

We sing "Onward Christian Soldiers" and wait to be drafted.

We sing "Oh, for a Thousand Tongues to Sing" and don't use the ones we have to speak for Christ.

We sing "Blest Be the Tie" and let the slightest offense sever it.

We sing "I Love to Tell the Story" and seldom mention Jesus to anybody.

We sing "Serve the Lord with Gladness" and gripe about all we have to do.

We sing "Cast Thy Burden on the Lord" and then worry ourselves into a nervous breakdown.

We sing "The Whole Wide World for Jesus" and never invite our next-door neighbor to church.

## 169. SING UNTO THE LORD

The meal had just been completed when one person rose from the table and led the group in a hymn. The disciples were not greatly surprised when Jesus announced that they would sing a psalm. The simple words of Matthew, "They sang a hymn," tell with eloquence that the disciples responded to Jesus' request.

Today we sing hymns as a part of our worship services. What do you do when the music director announces a hymn? What would you have done had you been present with Jesus on that memorable night when He announced the hymn? Would you have remained silent, or would you have joined reverently with the others?

## 170. PARABLE OF A CHURCH CHOIR

A certain choir director considered one Sunday how many of the gifted singers in the church were in the pews instead of the choir loft. Their voices, although they were gifts of God, were not bearing fruit.

And the choir director thought to himself, "They might as well be deprived of their voices because they will not sing."

But the Master Chorister spoke to the choir director and said, "Wish them not the loss of their voices. Tell them again of their responsibility to use their talents in My house. I will speak to them through My special Messenger and prick their consciences. Give them another chance to sing praises to Me."

And another chance was offered the inactive singers to be fruitful. Some rededicated their talents to God and bore fruit. But some refused to sing; and behold, their voices withered and disappeared. (With apologies to Luke 13:6-9).

# 12
# Home and Family Life

## 171. TEN COMMANDMENTS FOR PARENTS

1. Thou shalt guard thy children in thy home and on the street.
2. Thou shalt make thy home a sanctuary of love and devotion.
3. Thou shalt honor the teachers of thy children and teach thy children to honor them.
4. Thou shalt not condone the faults of thy children through a misguided sense of family loyalty.
5. Thou shalt teach thy children respect for the law and keep them from the companionship of children who are disrespectful of the law.
6. Thou shalt not lead thy children into temptation by providing them with too much money or too many earthly possessions.
7. Thou shalt enforce decency in the dress of thy children.
8. Thou shalt protect the morals of thy children from the indiscretion of youthful ardor and inexperience.
9. Thou shalt not judge thy children according to the standards of adult behavior.

10. Thou shalt conduct thyself in such a manner as to set an example worthy of imitation by thy children.

## 172. HOW TO RAISE A WAYWARD CHILD

1. Never eat together as a family.
2. Never have traditional family activities that your children look forward to.
3. Never listen to your children; talk at them, not to them.
4. Never let your children experience cold, fatigue, adventure, injury, risk, challenge, experimentation, failure, frustration, or discouragement.
5. Warn your children of the dangers of drugs while you drink alcohol and smoke cigarettes.
6. Never give your children any meaningful spiritual training. Instead, emphasize religious ritual, outward appearances, and the letter of the law.
7. Always prefer material pursuits to family activities.
8. Continually tell others what great things your children are doing—and always expect them to win.
9. Disobey the law in front of your children and tell them by your attitude that the laws were passed for everyone but you.
10. Never correct your children. Always assume that they are right and everyone else is wrong.
11. Always pick up after your children; never given them any responsibility.
12. Always solve your children's problems and make their decisions for them.

## 173. THE PARENTS' BEATITUDES

Blessed are the parents who make their peace with spilled milk and mud, for of such is the kingdom of childhood.

Blessed are the parents who refuse to compare their children with others, for precious unto each is the rhythm of his own growth.

Blessed are the fathers and mothers who have learned to laugh, for it is the music of the child's world.

Blessed are those parents who understand the goodness of time, for they make it not a sword that kills growth but a shield to protect and guide their children.

Blessed are the parents who can say no without anger, for comforting to the child is the security of a firm decision.

Blessed are the parents who treat their children consistently, for this makes children secure.

Blessed are those parents who accept the awkwardness of their growing children, letting each grow at his own speed.

Blessed are the parents who are teachable, for knowledge brings understanding and understanding brings love.

Blessed are the parents who love their children in the midst of a hostile world, for love is the greatest of all gifts.

## 174. THE PARENT'S PRAYER

O Master, make me a better parent. Teach me to understand my children, to listen patiently to what they say, and to answer all their questions kindly. Keep me from interrupting them, talking back to them, and contradicting them. Make me as courteous to them as I want them to be to me. Give me the courage to confess my sins against my children and to ask their forgiveness when I know that I have wronged them.

May I not hurt the feelings of my children. Forbid that I should laugh at their mistakes or ridicule them as punishment. Let me not tempt them to lie and steal. Guide me hour by hour that I may demonstrate by all I say and do that honesty produces happiness.

Blind me to the little errors of my children, and help me to see the good things that they do. Give me a ready word for honest praise when they do right.

Help me to grow up with my children, to treat them as children and not as adults. Let me not judge them according to the standards of adult behavior. Do not allow me to rob them of the opportunity to wait upon themselves, to think, to choose, and to make decisions.

Forbid that I should ever punish them for my own selfish satisfaction. May I grant them all their wishes that are reasonable and have the courage always to withhold a privilege which I know will harm them.

Make me so fair and just, so considerate and compassionate to my children, that they will have a genuine esteem for me. Make me worthy of being loved and imitated by my children.

## 175. WHAT I WANT MY CHILDREN TO REMEMBER ABOUT OUR HOME

That their father and mother loved each other.

That our home was a happy one because we all worked to keep it that way.

That each child was given every possible opportunity to develop his own personality.

That each child's personal possessions were sacred to him if kept in their proper place.

That the books in the house were to be read (and handled rightly), and that none were under lock and key because of questionable contents.

That absolute truth abided there; no earnest questioner, however young, was put off with evasion and excuses.

That we practiced hospitality, and that our friends loved to visit us.

That Sunday was the happiest day of the week, one which we all looked forward to because it was the day when we went to church together.

That although father and mother worked hard and long at their respective jobs, they found time every day to keep informed on current events, to read good books, to have fun with their children, and to pray.

# 13
# Youth and
# Their Needs

## 176. HOW TO GET ALONG WITH YOUR PARENTS

Don't be afraid to speak their language. Try using strange words and phrases like "I'll help wash the dishes," "yes," "thank you," and "please."

Try to understand their music. Play Glenn Miller's "Moonlight Serenade" on the stereo and accustom yourself to the strange sound.

Be patient with the underachiever. When you catch your dieting mom sneaking salted nuts, don't show your disapproval. Tell her you like fat mothers.

Encourage them to talk about their problems. Try to keep in mind that things like earning a living and paying off the mortgage are important to them. Be tolerant about their appearance. When your dad gets a haircut, don't feel personally humiliated. Remember, it's important to him to look like his peers.

And most important of all: If they do something you consider wrong, let them know it's their behavior you dislike, not them. Remember, parents need to feel loved!

## 177. TEN THINGS I WISH I HAD KNOWN BEFORE I WAS TWENTY-ONE

1. That being a Christian is really important.
2. That my life's vocation would be what it is.
3. That my health after thirty would depend to a great degree on what I ate before I was twenty-one.
4. That I am really a trustee of my money and possessions.
5. That being neatly and sensibly dressed is an asset.
6. That habits are mighty hard to change after you're twenty-one.
7. That worthwhile things require time, patience, and work.
8. That the world gives a person just about what he deserves.
9. That a thorough education brings not only better wages, but the best of everything.
10. That absolute truthfulness in everything is invaluable.
11. And one more for extra thought: That my parents weren't "old fogies" after all!

## 178. TEN COMMANDMENTS FOR TEENAGERS

The following "Ten Commandments for Teenagers" were adopted by four thousand student delegates to the Federation of High Schools convention in San Francisco several years ago:

1. Stop and think before you drink.
2. Don't let your parents down; they brought you up.
3. Be humble enough to obey. You will be giving orders yourself some day.
4. At the first temptation, turn away from unclean thinking.
5. Don't show off when driving. If you want to race, go to the track.
6. Date those who would make a good mate.
7. Go to church faithfully. The Creator gave us the week; give him back at least an hour.

116

8. Choose your companions carefully. You are what they are.
9. Avoid following the crowd. Be an engine, not a caboose.
10. Best of all, keep the original Ten Commandments.

# 14
# The Pastor and
# His Work

## 179. WHAT TO DO FOR YOUR PASTOR

Build his **spiritual power** by praying for him. When you pray for your pastor, you pray for your church, your community, and your family.

Build his **reputation** by speaking well of him. All pastors are human; they have weak and strong points. His influence will depend on which of them you stress.

Build his **morale** by encouraging him. Every pastor needs to be encouraged at times. Encouragement costs so little, yet it means so much!

Build his **leadership** by cooperating with him. For every great leader, there must be some great followers.

Build his **pulpit power** by coming to hear him. Full pews challenge a pastor to prepare and deliver great sermons. Empty pews can discourage him.

By far the greatest thing you can do for your pastor is to follow the Christ whom he preaches and exemplifies.

## 180. THE FAITHFUL PASTOR

*He holds the lamp each Sabbath day*
*So low that none could miss the way;*
*And yet so high to bring in sight*
*That picture fair, of Christ the light,*
*That gazing up, the lamp between,*
*The hand that holds it is not seen.*

*He holds the pitcher, stooping low*
*To lips of little ones below;*
*Then raises it to the weary saint*
*And bids him drink when sick and faint.*
*They drink, the pitcher thus between,*
*The hand that holds it scarce is seen.*

*He blows the trumpet, soft and clear,*
*That trembling sinners need not fear;*
*And then with louder note and bold,*
*To storm the walls of Satan's hold;*
*The trumpet coming thus between,*
*The hand that holds it is not seen.*

*But when our captain says, "Well done,*
*Thou good and faithful servant! Come!*
*Lay down the pitcher and the lamp,*
*Lay down the trumpet; leave the camp";*
*His weary hands will then be seen*
*In the hands of Christ—nothing between.*

## 181. THE PASTOR'S WIFE

*There is one person in our church*
*Who knows our pastor's life,*
*Who weeps and smiles and prays with him—*
*And that's the pastor's wife.*

*The crowd had seen him in his strength*
*When wielding God's sharp sword,*
*As underneath God's banner's folds*
*He faced the devil's horde.*

*But deep within her heart she knows*
*That scarce an hour before,*
*She helped him pray the glory down*
*Behind the closet door.*

*She's heard him groaning in his soul*
*When bitter raged the strife,*
*As, hand in hand, she knelt with him—*
*For she's the pastor's wife!*

*You tell your tales of prophets brave*
*Who marched across the world*
*And changed the course of history*
*By burning words they hurled.*

*And I will tell how back of each*
*Some woman lived her life;*
*Who wept with him and smiled with him—*
*She was the pastor's wife!*

## 182. A PRAYER FOR MY PASTOR

Father, let me be a pillar of strength to help hold up my pastor and not a thorn in his flesh to sap his strength, or a burden on his back to weigh him down.

Let me support him without striving to possess him. Let me lift his hands without shackling them. Let me give him any help that he may devote more time to working for the salvation of others and less time to gratifying my vanity.

Let me work for him as the pastor of all the members and not compel him to spend precious time in pleasing me. Let me be unselfish in what I do for him and in what I ask him to do for me.

## 183. ENCOURAGE YOUR PASTOR

*If you like the pastor's sermons,*
*Why not stop and tell him so?*

It will give him inspiration—
    More than you will ever know.

If you like the work he's doing,
    Do not be afraid to say;
It will give him added courage
    For the burden of the day.

If you think he's being partial
    To some members of his flock,
He is merely being friendly—
    Do not start a lot of talk!

Just remember he has trials,
    Just the same as you and I;
Though he can't please all the people,
    Neither could our Lord on high.

If you have a word of kindness—
    Not a lot of flowery praise—
You should let your pastor know it;
    It will brighten up his days.

# 15
# Christianity and Christian Influence

## 184. CHRIST, THE ONLY WAY

Indulgence says, "Drink your way out."
Philosophy says, "Think your way out."
Science says, "Invent your way out."
Industry says, "Work your way out."
Communism says, "Strike your way out."
Fascism says, "Bluff your way out."
Militarism says, "Fight your way out."
But Christ says, "I am the way out."

## 185. DEFINITION OF A CHRISTIAN

A Christian is:

A **mind** through which Christ thinks.

A **heart** through which Christ loves.

A **voice** through which Christ speaks.

A **hand** through which Christ helps.

## 186. WHAT IT MEANS TO BE A CHRISTIAN

A Christian is slow to lose patience and quick to be gracious.

A Christian looks for a way to be constructive, even when provoked.

A Christian refrains from trying to impress others with his own importance.

A Christian practices good manners.

A Christian is not "touchy," even when insulted.

A Christian thinks the best, not the worst, of others. He is wise as a serpent and harmless as a dove in dealing with others.

A Christian does not gloat over the wickedness of other people.

Above all else, a Christian exhibits the love of Christ in his heart and life.


## 187. DEFINITION OF THE GOSPEL

Our gospel is:
    Joyful in tone.
    Earnest in spirit.
    Satisfying to the soul.
    Uplifting to all.
    Sane in its appeal.


## 188. HOW TO BUILD UP THE CAUSE OF CHRIST

Christians need to:
    Wake up,
    Sing up,
    Preach up,
    Pray up,
    Stay up,

Pay up,
But never give up,
Let up,
Back up,
Shut up—
Until the cause of Christ and the church in the world is built up.

## 189. I SHALL NOT PASS THIS WAY AGAIN

I expect to pass through this world but once. Any good, therefore, that I can do, or any kindness that I can show to any fellow being, let me do it now. Let me not defer it or neglect it, for I shall not pass this way again.

## 190. MY INFLUENCE

*My life shall touch a dozen lives*
*Before this day is done;*
*Leave countless marks for good or ill,*
*Ere sets the evening sun.*

*So this the wish I always wish,*
*The prayer I ever pray;*
*"Lord, may my life help other lives*
*It touches by the way."*

# 16
# Christian Leadership

## 191. THE MEANING OF CHURCH LEADERSHIP

Loyal. A leader sets an example in loyalty to the whole church program.

Enterprising. A leader is industrious and sees through or around difficulties. He does not mind working hard and sacrificially.

Attentive. A leader gives close attention to details, remembering that "cursed is he that doeth the work of the Lord negligently."

Dependable. A leader is always ready and on time. He is always present not only for the service for which he is responsible but for all services.

Eager. A leader is enthusiastic about serving the Lord in the position to which he has been elected.

Radiant. A leader is happy and optimistic, seldom criticizing and always encouraging others.

Surrendered. A leader puts Christ first, others second, and himself last.

Honest. A leader gives at least one-seventh of his time and one-tenth of his money to the Lord through his church.

Industrious. A leader works hard. He matches talk with real work, week by week.

Prayerful. A leader serves as if everything depended on him and prays as if everything depended on God.

## 192. BEATITUDES FOR CHURCH LEADERS

Blessed is the leader who has not sought the highest places but who has been drafted into them because of his ability and willingness to serve.

Blessed is the leader who knows where he is going, why he is going, and how to get there.

Blessed is the leader who knows no discouragement and presents no alibi.

Blessed is the leader who can lead without being dictatorial.

Blessed is the leader who seeks the best for those whom he serves.

Blessed is the leader who leads for the good of the majority and not for himself.

Blessed is the leader who marches with the group and interprets the signs that lead to success.

Blessed is the leader who considers leadership to be Christian service.

Blessed is the leader who is eager to train for his office.

# 17
# Ministering
# to Others

---

## 193. A DEFINITION OF LOVE

Love is:

Writing a letter of appreciation to someone.

Taking flowers, food, or other needed items to shut-ins or the sick.

Expressing sympathy to those in sorrow.

Making the way easier for Christians who are trying to live right.

Offering to bring someone to Sunday school and church.

In short, love is Christian care and compassion in action.

## 194. A GIFT FOR MY NEIGHBOR

*If my neighbor needed a cup of sugar,*
*I would give it to him;*
*But what if he needed a friend?*

*If my neighbor needed bread,*
*I would share with him;*
*But what if he needed love?*

*If my neighbor needed shoes,*
*I would provide them for him;*
*But what if he needed compassion?*

*If my neighbor needed water,*
*I would dig him a well;*
*But what if he needed God?*

*God grant me the wisdom*
*To give my neighbor*
*What he really needs!*

## 195. A TEA PARTY FOR ME

In order to minister to other people, we have to give ourselves. Perhaps too many of us have the selfish attitude reflected in this poem:

*I had a little tea party*
*This afternoon at three.*
*'Twas very small—*
*Three guests in all—*
*Just I, myself, and me.*
*Myself ate all the sandwiches,*
*While I drank up the tea;*
*'Twas also I who ate the pie*
*And passed the cake to me.*

A person all wrapped up in himself cannot share himself with other people. Only Christ can deliver us from our selfishness and open our eyes to the needs of others.

## 196. THE NEEDS OF THE WORLD

I planned a modern home, but a Korean citizen whispered, "I have no home at all."

I dreamed of a country place for the pleasure of my children, but an exiled lad kept saying, "I have no country."

I picked out a new china cabinet, but a child in China cried out, "I have no cup."

I started to buy a new washing machine, but a Polish woman said, "I have nothing to wash."

I wanted a large freezer, but across the water came the cry, "I have no food."

I ordered a new car for the pleasure of my family, but a war orphan cried, "I have no family."

I planned a stained glass window for my church, but a mission pastor murmured, "My church has no walls."

# 18
# Humor

---

### 197. HOW TO SCATTER A CROWD

When Theodore Roosevelt was police commissioner of New York City, he asked a job applicant what he would do if ordered to disperse a mob.

The man replied, "Pass around the hat, sir."

### 198. AN HONEST MAN

One outspoken pastor announced from his pulpit one Sunday morning: "Brethren, the janitor and I will hold our weekly prayer meeting next Wednesday night as usual."

### 199. A PRAYER WITH TEETH IN IT

The old evangelist Bud Robinson is reported to have prayed the following prayer each day: "O Lord, give me a backbone as big as a saw log and ribs like the sleepers under the church floor. Put iron shoes on my feet and galvanized breeches on my body. Give me a rhinoceros hide for skin, and hang up a wagonload of determination in the gable-end of my soul. Help me to sign the contract to fight the devil as long as I've got a tooth—and then gum him until I die."

## 200. SPACE TALK FOR CHURCHES

**All systems go**—The Sunday morning service is about to begin.

**Age of space**—The auditorium on Sunday night.

**Artificial gravity**—The look on everyone's face when the pastor announces he's going to preach on tithing.

**Burned-out booster**—The preacher about 10 P.M. on Sunday night.

**Did you read me?**—What the discarded church bulletin might say if it were alive.

**Echo 1, echo 2**—The preacher's jokes.

**Escape velocity**—The speed at which people leave the church on Sunday morning.

**Extravehicular activity**—Errands the pastor runs for church members.

**G force**—The pressure exerted by a soloist who wants to sing.

**Ground zero**—The pulpit.

**Joint cooperation in space**—Congregational singing.

**Parent craft**—Learning to get along with the parents of your Sunday school children.

**Return to earth**—The preacher standing at the door after the service.

**Scrubbed**—Visitation called off due to lack of interest.

**Surveyor**—Pulpit committee.

**Ten-minute hold**—The invitation.

**Walking in space**—What some church members think the preacher ought to do—all the time.          —*Bennie Rhodes*

# Record
## of Publication

| Item No. | Where Published | When Published |
| --- | --- | --- |
| | | |
| | | |
| | | |
| | | |
| | | |
| | | |
| | | |
| | | |
| | | |
| | | |

| Item No. | Where Published | When Published |
|---|---|---|
| ____ | _____ | ____ |
| ____ | _____ | ____ |
| ____ | _____ | ____ |
| ____ | _____ | ____ |
| ____ | _____ | ____ |
| ____ | _____ | ____ |
| ____ | _____ | ____ |
| ____ | _____ | ____ |
| ____ | _____ | ____ |
| ____ | _____ | ____ |
| ____ | _____ | ____ |
| ____ | _____ | ____ |
| ____ | _____ | ____ |
| ____ | _____ | ____ |
| ____ | _____ | ____ |
| ____ | _____ | ____ |
| ____ | _____ | ____ |
| ____ | _____ | ____ |
| ____ | _____ | ____ |

| Item No. | Where Published | When Published |
|----------|-----------------|----------------|
| ———      | ————————————    | ————           |
| ———      | ————————————    | ————           |
| ———      | ————————————    | ————           |
| ———      | ————————————    | ————           |
| ———      | ————————————    | ————           |
| ———      | ————————————    | ————           |
| ———      | ————————————    | ————           |
| ———      | ————————————    | ————           |
| ———      | ————————————    | ————           |
| ———      | ————————————    | ————           |
| ———      | ————————————    | ————           |
| ———      | ————————————    | ————           |
| ———      | ————————————    | ————           |
| ———      | ————————————    | ————           |
| ———      | ————————————    | ————           |
| ———      | ————————————    | ————           |
| ———      | ————————————    | ————           |
| ———      | ————————————    | ————           |
| ———      | ————————————    | ————           |

| Item No. | Where Published | When Published |
|----------|-----------------|----------------|
| _____ | _____ | _____ |
| _____ | _____ | _____ |
| _____ | _____ | _____ |
| _____ | _____ | _____ |
| _____ | _____ | _____ |
| _____ | _____ | _____ |
| _____ | _____ | _____ |
| _____ | _____ | _____ |
| _____ | _____ | _____ |
| _____ | _____ | _____ |
| _____ | _____ | _____ |
| _____ | _____ | _____ |
| _____ | _____ | _____ |
| _____ | _____ | _____ |
| _____ | _____ | _____ |
| _____ | _____ | _____ |
| _____ | _____ | _____ |
| _____ | _____ | _____ |
| _____ | _____ | _____ |

| Item No. | Where Published | When Published |
|---|---|---|
| _____ | _____ | _____ |
| _____ | _____ | _____ |
| _____ | _____ | _____ |
| _____ | _____ | _____ |
| _____ | _____ | _____ |
| _____ | _____ | _____ |
| _____ | _____ | _____ |
| _____ | _____ | _____ |
| _____ | _____ | _____ |
| _____ | _____ | _____ |
| _____ | _____ | _____ |
| _____ | _____ | _____ |
| _____ | _____ | _____ |
| _____ | _____ | _____ |
| _____ | _____ | _____ |
| _____ | _____ | _____ |
| _____ | _____ | _____ |
| _____ | _____ | _____ |
| _____ | _____ | _____ |
| _____ | _____ | _____ |

| Item No. | Where Published | When Published |
|----------|-----------------|----------------|
| _____  | _____ | _____ |
| _____  | _____ | _____ |
| _____  | _____ | _____ |
| _____  | _____ | _____ |
| _____  | _____ | _____ |
| _____  | _____ | _____ |
| _____  | _____ | _____ |
| _____  | _____ | _____ |
| _____  | _____ | _____ |
| _____  | _____ | _____ |
| _____  | _____ | _____ |
| _____  | _____ | _____ |
| _____  | _____ | _____ |
| _____  | _____ | _____ |
| _____  | _____ | _____ |
| _____  | _____ | _____ |
| _____  | _____ | _____ |
| _____  | _____ | _____ |
| _____  | _____ | _____ |

| Item No. | Where Published | When Published |
|---|---|---|
| _____ | _____ | _____ |
| _____ | _____ | _____ |
| _____ | _____ | _____ |
| _____ | _____ | _____ |
| _____ | _____ | _____ |
| _____ | _____ | _____ |
| _____ | _____ | _____ |
| _____ | _____ | _____ |
| _____ | _____ | _____ |
| _____ | _____ | _____ |
| _____ | _____ | _____ |
| _____ | _____ | _____ |
| _____ | _____ | _____ |
| _____ | _____ | _____ |
| _____ | _____ | _____ |
| _____ | _____ | _____ |
| _____ | _____ | _____ |
| _____ | _____ | _____ |
| _____ | _____ | _____ |
| _____ | _____ | _____ |

| Item No. | Where Published | When Published |
|----------|-----------------|----------------|
| _____ | _____ | _____ |
| _____ | _____ | _____ |
| _____ | _____ | _____ |
| _____ | _____ | _____ |
| _____ | _____ | _____ |
| _____ | _____ | _____ |
| _____ | _____ | _____ |
| _____ | _____ | _____ |
| _____ | _____ | _____ |
| _____ | _____ | _____ |
| _____ | _____ | _____ |
| _____ | _____ | _____ |
| _____ | _____ | _____ |
| _____ | _____ | _____ |
| _____ | _____ | _____ |
| _____ | _____ | _____ |
| _____ | _____ | _____ |
| _____ | _____ | _____ |
| _____ | _____ | _____ |

| Item No. | Where Published | When Published |
|----------|-----------------|----------------|
| _____ | _____ | _____ |
| _____ | _____ | _____ |
| _____ | _____ | _____ |
| _____ | _____ | _____ |
| _____ | _____ | _____ |
| _____ | _____ | _____ |
| _____ | _____ | _____ |
| _____ | _____ | _____ |
| _____ | _____ | _____ |
| _____ | _____ | _____ |
| _____ | _____ | _____ |
| _____ | _____ | _____ |
| _____ | _____ | _____ |
| _____ | _____ | _____ |
| _____ | _____ | _____ |
| _____ | _____ | _____ |
| _____ | _____ | _____ |
| _____ | _____ | _____ |
| _____ | _____ | _____ |
| _____ | _____ | _____ |

| Item No. | Where Published | When Published |
|---|---|---|
| _____ | _____ | _____ |
| _____ | _____ | _____ |
| _____ | _____ | _____ |
| _____ | _____ | _____ |
| _____ | _____ | _____ |
| _____ | _____ | _____ |
| _____ | _____ | _____ |
| _____ | _____ | _____ |
| _____ | _____ | _____ |
| _____ | _____ | _____ |
| _____ | _____ | _____ |
| _____ | _____ | _____ |
| _____ | _____ | _____ |
| _____ | _____ | _____ |
| _____ | _____ | _____ |
| _____ | _____ | _____ |
| _____ | _____ | _____ |
| _____ | _____ | _____ |
| _____ | _____ | _____ |

| Item No. | Where Published | When Published |
|----------|-----------------|----------------|
|          |                 |                |
|          |                 |                |
|          |                 |                |
|          |                 |                |
|          |                 |                |
|          |                 |                |
|          |                 |                |
|          |                 |                |
|          |                 |                |
|          |                 |                |
|          |                 |                |
|          |                 |                |
|          |                 |                |
|          |                 |                |
|          |                 |                |
|          |                 |                |
|          |                 |                |
|          |                 |                |
|          |                 |                |
|          |                 |                |